Anonymous

**Japanese Women**

Anonymous

**Japanese Women**

ISBN/EAN: 9783337175375

Printed in Europe, USA, Canada, Australia, Japan

Cover: Foto ©Suzi / pixelio.de

More available books at **www.hansebooks.com**

# JAPANESE WOMEN

# JAPANESE WOMEN.

PRIVATELY PRINTED BY
A. C. McClurg & Company,
CHICAGO
FOR

## THE JAPANESE WOMAN'S COMMISSION

FOR THE

## WORLD'S COLUMBIAN EXPOSITION,

CHICAGO, ILL., U. S. A.

1893.

# PREFACE.

In accordance with the invitation of the Board of Lady Managers of the World's Columbian Commission, for the grand scheme of exhibiting Woman's work in general, the Japanese Woman's Commission for this Exposition was organized under the co-operation of several noble ladies, and the works resulting from the hands of the Japanese Women have been exhibited. Taking advantage of this precious opportunity, the Commission desires and aims, in this work, to present to the world's public, however briefly, the true condition of the Japanese woman, ancient and modern.

This work has been written by several authoresses, each chapter being undertaken by a different lady who is especially interested in and perfectly informed of the subject assigned to her.

THE JAPANESE WOMAN'S COMMISSION

FOR THE

WORLD'S COLUMBIAN EXPOSITION,

CHICAGO, ILLINOIS, U. S. A.

1893.

# TABLE OF CONTENTS.

# Japanese Women.

# CHAPTER I

## INTRÒDUCTION.

Japan, superficially, is now pretty well known to the world, but as regards her internal affairs she still remains quite a dark country to the Occident. Her women, for instance, are misunderstood to a great extent, for it is impossible that visitors who have hitherto written upon Japan could see them in their true light, without any acquaintance with their homes. We, therefore, publish this pamphlet to place them just as they are before the eyes of the world on this occasion of the World's Fair. It must be understood, however, that this small treatise cannot but leave many points untouched.

How do the Japanese women compare with their American or European sisters? This question it is our object to answer, not by means of argument or criticism, but by a series of facts, which will enable readers to judge for themselves.

Firstly, we shall speak of Japanese women in political affairs. Their interference in them was sometimes for good, and at other times for evil. Our politics were by no means free from certain well-known evils, produced by their interference, but we will pay more attention to the good results effected by their political acts. Women used to play an important part on the political stage in ancient times. This is, indeed, one of the reasons why women were in general highly esteemed in old Japan.

Secondly, of the contribution of women to literature, and their standing in the lettered community.

Thirdly, of what women have done in religion, as patrons and votaries.

Fourthly, of the domestic life of women, as daughters, wives and mothers.

Fifthly, of the industries of women.

Sixthly, of the accomplishments of women, such as music, tea-making (*tencha*), incense burning (*ko*), flower arranging (*ikebana*), painting, etc.

Seventhly and lastly, of their present educational and benevolent labors.

The first three chapters deal with historical facts and the rest with the present condition of things.

Rich as this country is in ancient records, those which pertain to women are very scarce, and it is no light work to make up their history. This is no doubt due, on one hand, to the secret nature of womanly interference, and on the other, to the delicate modesty of our women.

Before taking up the topics above mentioned let us trace the gradations through which Japanese women have come to be what they are, both as regards morality and social position. Little is, of course, known of our primitive mothers. It may, however, be proved almost beyond a doubt that women were highly esteemed in the days of old, until the introduction of Chinese manners and institutions and of Buddhism made it fashionable to depreciate them. But fashion could work only on the surface of things, and that only for a short space of time.

As time went on, scholars and artists appeared among them and their influence was felt, especially at all social gatherings. The court ladies were very influential and respected on account of their skill in poetry, which has been from time immemorial one of the most cherished accomplishments of the Imperial court. In the tenth and eleventh centuries court ladies were such excellent poetesses that they had no equals in our history. They stood, indeed, on an equality with men in the estimation of society.

From the *Genji-Monogatari*, a novel by Murasaki Shikibu, who lived when female culture was so high, we can gain considerable insight into the women of those times. We there see them described something like the following:

4

They were mistresses of feminine accomplishments, as music, literature, painting, chirography, incense burning, etc. In literature they paid by far the greatest attention to Japanese poems. It was held unwomanly to learn Chinese, and even those who had some knowledge of it tried assiduously to conceal it. But it was not rare among gentlewomen to read Buddhist sutras in Chinese, from which was drawn their moral codes. They strictly observed the rules of etiquette. They paid much attention to the toilet. They practiced sewing, dyeing and weaving as well as cooking, from the highest woman to the humblest girl. In every family it was their duty to decorate the rooms, especially on ceremonial occasions. It was their part to educate the girls. They freely mingled in society and were, in consequence, bright and charming, not like their descendants, whose shyness and reserve are almost proverbial. However, they held nothing so bad as to put on airs and to let their tongues glide too freely. They were severely warned against boasting of their learning. Murasaki Shikibu, herself, who was a profound scholar, is said to have looked like one ignorant of even the numerical figures.

Chastity was held their prime virtue. So much was it respected that no woman, however beautiful and accomplished, could find a husband, if her character was at all questionable.

Jealousy was considered the vilest of female vices. Murasaki Shikibu strongly writes against becoming its slave, while giving some very pointed remarks as to how wives should endeavor to please their husbands and make them love their homes.

It was the duty of wives not only to make pleasant homes, but to aid their husbands in public concerns by means of advice. Thus their standing was very high and they were looked up to as model women for many succeeding generations. We find a discipline laid down for women by Abutsuni, in her letter to her daughter, who was a court lady in the middle of the thirteenth century, nearly equal to that embodied by Murasaki Shikibu in her novel. This letter states in full what a woman should do and should be. Here follow some of the most important points of the letter:

5

"A woman's education need not go beyond writing, drawing, music, incense burning, history, novels and poetry."

"Avoid doing whatever tends to make others censure you, however highly you may regard it. A woman should try to charm with her heart and mind, not with her beauty or accomplishments."

"Strive to be older than your age without being precocious, for precocity is by no means amiable."

"Hold it of little use to have many friends. A few select ones will suffice. Think twice before you take pleasure in light friendship. Love hearts, not outward appearances, natural gifts or accomplishments. In the exchange of friendly tokens, never be too warm, nor too cool, nor too pushing, nor too reserved. Bear in mind you will be known by your friends."

"I will tell you once for all that nothing is so rare as a true friend."

"It is the happiest life to live at home under the care of parents. Court life, full as it is of pleasure, has its share of pains. It often taxes moral courage to its very extremity. At court hold strictly to loyalty."

"The spring flowers and autumn maples you may enjoy or not, but do not forget to contemplate the frost-bitten plants of winter. Nothing so eloquently tells us how vain is this world. Weed out impure thoughts as they spring up in your mind."

"Our life is but a short-lived dream. Study carefully the Buddhist doctrine, and let not worldly pains and troubles torment you."

Rules were also for etiquette and the toilet, but these do not bear directly upon our subject.

This was not the first time that Buddhism was made the instrument for eradicating bad thoughts and inordinate intentions. Buddhism had begun to control the mind of women as well as men, long before the time of Abutsuni.

The fourteenth, fifteenth and sixteenth centuries saw a series of revolutions, which resulted in the establishment of the feudal system. The interests of women had been utterly neglected during those 300 years, and when peace returned, with Tokugawa holding the reins of government, Confucianism quickly grew in influence. The standard of morality was accordingly changed, but the influence of women, which had sunk during the stormy centuries, could not at once be revived, as, by the doctrine of Confucius, women were considered of but little importance.

In the seventeenth century there appeared many great Confucian scholars, of whom some directed their attention to female education. One of them was Nakamura Tekisai, who wrote the *Himekagami* or 'ladies' mirror;' another, Fujii Ransai, who wrote the *Fujin Oshiyegusa* or 'teachings for women;' another, Otakasaka Shizan, whose wife wrote the *Kara-Nishiki* or 'Chinese brocade;' another and the greatest, Kaibara Ekken, of whose teachings a lengthened account will presently follow.

The teachings of these scholars were all based upon the doctrines of the great Chinese sage, and were far different from those contained in the *Genji-Monogatari*. Formerly women had had their minds filled and cultured by reading novels, histories and poems, mostly from the pen of their own sex, and their souls consoled by the teachings of Buddhist priests. But now that unlettered warriors took to the rearrangement of society and the rising scholars taught in opposition to Buddhism, it is no wonder that a rather too strict moral code was established for women. This code, with its advantages and disadvantages, has since governed Japanese women. Its main point will, therefore, be mentioned here. For so doing, we will follow Kaibara Ekken's 'Female Education,' as we have no better way at our command.

Ekken based his work on female education upon the books of Confucius, especially the *Shogaku;* or, "Elements of Learning," by Shuki; and the *Jokai;* or, "Exhortation to Women," by So Taiko.

To give the chief points of his system:

1. Girls will be educated the best at home by their parents. They need only to learn elementary lessons in writing, reading and arithmetic. They should be taught in pure old Japanese poems and of some Chinese classics, such as the opening chapters of the *Kokyo* and *Rongo*, So Taiko's *Jokn*, and others calculated to give them the best rules for obedience and chastity.

2. They should be taught in the various domestic duties, such as weaving, sewing, washing and cooking.

Ekken aimed at practical good and therefore did not attach much importance to music.

His moral code was very comprehensive, and contained many rules applicable to men, but for girls only those are enumerated suitable for their future lives as wives and mothers.

A woman should not follow her own thoughts. It is her duty simply to obey—obey her parents while young; obey her husband when married; obey her children in old age. These are the Joshino Sanjiu; or, "*The Three Obediences.*"

7

3. A woman should guard against loquacity, should select her words with care, and utter none of bad meaning.

4. A woman should take especial care of her deportment, watching lest it become manly or rude.

5. A woman should be neat in her person and garments.

6. A woman should not neglect domestic duties from dawn till night. The futoku, *'female virtue'* (3); the fugen, *'female words'* (4); the fuyo, *'female appearance'* (5 and 6), and the fuko, *'female works'* (7). These are called " *The Four Female Duties,*" none of which should be slighted by a woman.

7. A married woman should consider her husband the only heaven to look up to, and serve him as if he were her master.

8. A wife should serve not only her husband but his parents, respecting them more than her own, and consulting their pleasure before she does anything out of her daily routine. She should not be irritated even though they treat her rather unkindly. This is for the sake of a peaceable home.

9. A wife should pay due respect to her husband's brothers and sisters and other relatives; or she will lose not only their love, but the love of her parents.

It was then customary for a woman, as it is to a great extent at present, to marry a husband chosen by her parents, not by herself. A woman was supposed to have had no home before marriage. In other words, to marry was, on her part, to return home. Once married, she had no home to return to. To add to her helplessness she had no right of calling anything her own, her body and mind not excepted. Moreover, divorce, whether active or passive, was the height of disgrace for a woman. Thus everything was planned so that a wife should wholly depend upon her husband.

A wife was obliged, as she is at present, to live in her husband's house with his parents, brothers and sisters, as it was held a duty for a grown son to support his aged parents and to live under the same roof with them.

In order that she might the more easily adapt herself to her complex home, Ekken urges every woman to sacrifice herself as much as possible in all her duties. Finally Ekken enumerates what he called the five moral diseases of women and strongly warned them against these infirmities. They are: *a.* Disobedience.

*b.* Anger and hate.

*c.* Slander.

*d.* Envy

*e.* Ignorance.

8

He says: "Most women have one or more of these diseases, thereby making themselves inferior to men. They ought to strive to get rid of them.

"The most important of these five diseases is ignorance, it being in most cases the cause of others.

"Women are inferior to men in general knowledge and wisdom. It rarely happens that they see at first sight, what is clear to men of common sense, at once and suffer accordingly. They often speak ill of others without knowing that it produces results just contrary to their object, not only upon themselves but upon their husbands and children. Their blind love of their children often spoils the young minds.

"Therefore, I propose that women be educated so that they may not go astray from the path of moral purity."

Ekken was right in saying that women are more disposed to the five diseases than men, and that they must be educated with a special view to root them out. But his methods of education were of much too oppressing a nature to be suitable for making gentlewomen in the full sense of the word in this civilized age.

Ekken's system of education was in vogue during more than two hundred years of the Tokugawa's government, and it is much esteemed even at present by all educators of girls.

A book called the "Onna-Daigaku," an epitome of his system of education, was in use throughout the whole empire, as the copy-book for girl students in the feudal ages and in the first years of the Meiji period.

At present women in this empire are becoming more and more like their sisters in Europe and America. But as it is only twenty years or so, since foreign institutions and systems of education were introduced, the leading power in society is still in the hands of women educated under the old system. However, in a not far distant future ladies educated under the western systems will exert more and more influence.

9

# CHAPTER II.

# JAPANESE WOMEN IN POLITICS.

## INTRODUCTION.

A precept has been inculcated in this country from time immemorial, and, let us hope, is destined to continue for all ages to come, that men should concern themselves with matters outside their homes, and women with domestic affairs; that, in short, men should lead and women follow. Forward· ness on the part of women has consequently been vigorously suppressed by our countrymen. But in many things success depends upon proper harmony and co-operation between the members of the opposite sexes. There is no reason then, that women should be excluded altogether from the public affairs of the country. Indeed, although they have not always taken a direct part in politics, women have rendered, in every age, indirect services of high value to the State, as their husbands' helpmates and comforters, and as their sons' guides and instructresses. Instances are not wanting of women scoring rare success in the fields of peaceful administration as well as of warfare. The precept above alluded to is meant as a check upon such women as may be betrayed by their shallow wits, into acts of audacity and presumption to the detriment of the national interests. There have been women who have conducted the government of the country with eminent success ; women who took command in the fields of battle in the place of their brave husbands; women who have sacrificed themselves for the sake of their country; and finally, women who have consecrated their lives to works of charity and benevolence. But women being naturally shy and modest, the part their sex has played in the history of the country has not received that attention from historians to which they are fully entitled. It is our purpose in the following pages to make brief mention of a few of the more famous women, who have played distinguished parts in the political annals of the country.

## Remote Antiquity.

The precept as to the respective spheres of activity for men and women, to which reference has already been made, does not seem to have been vigorously applied in the remote ages of antiquity. The history of those times furnishes us with many instances of women assuming the reins of government. To begin with, Amaterasu Okami, otherwise called Hi-no Kami (Sun Goddess), daughter of Izanagi-no-Mikoto, is said to have been so wise and just that, as the ruler of Takama-ga Hara, she enjoyed the respect and admiration of all. She taught her people the arts of sericulture and weaving, and she also opened up the virgin plains of the Main Land of Japan. When she bequeathed her throne to her grandson, she gave him many valuable precepts as to the manner in which the gods should be worshiped, the relations between sovereign and subjects, and the relations between parents and children. It was she also who laid the foundation for the everlasting national polity of Japan. She is, indeed, revered as the founder of the country, and to her was offered the most respectful homage by the sovereigns of successive ages. The famous Shrine Naigu at Yamada, Ise, is dedicated to her memory.

The age in which she reigned being so remote, the knowledge we possess about her and her time is comparatively meager, and any minute account of her is of course entirely out of question. She belongs to the so-called Divine Ages (Kamiyo) of Japanese history. Coming down to the so-called Human Ages, it is to be noticed that women have been on the Throne of Japan altogether ten times. This list does not include the celebrated Empress Jingo, who, though for many years she exercised all the powers of a sovereign, had not the regal title. But her great achievements as well as her extraordinary gifts of nature, amply entitled her to a brief notice in this place. She was a woman of strong masculine character, with a genius for command and administration. She conquered Corea and gave a powerful impetus to the progress of civilization in Japan. Altogether she was an extraordinary woman. Her Corean invasion took place in 201 A. D. The southern portion of the peninsula comprising the countries of Kara and Mimana was at that time already in the possession of Japan. The country of Shiragi, which was adjacent to those just mentioned, did not acknowledge the authority of Japan and was in the habit of invading the territory of Kara. The Empress Jingo, consequently, went over primarily to chastise and conquer Shiragi, but she was able to extend Japanese sway over several other countries. From that time the whole of the southern half of the peninsula became tributary states to Japan; the northern half was still under the authority of China. Chinese civilization, which had for some time taken root in the Corean States, now freely found its way to this country, where it, in course of time, has developed into a new plant of great beauty and value. The Empress Jingo also fought some battles with princes, who contested the Throne with her own son. Subduing all rebellious pretenders to the Throne, she put her son upon it, she herself administering the government as Regent of the realm.

### Empresses.

In our country, it has been, and still is, the rule to select successors to the Throne from among the male members of the Imperial family, to the exclusion of female heirs. But this has not prevented, in unavoidable and exceptional cases, the occupation of the Throne by a member of the other sex. The first of the Empresses was Suiko.

The Empress Suiko was the daughter of the Emperor Kimmei, the twenty-ninth ruler after the great founder of the dynasty. Her name was Nukatabe no Miko. She was at first consort of the Emperor Bitatsu, her half brother, but soon becoming an Empress Dowager, she continued to wield, together with the Minister Umako, the real powers of sovereignty. After two Emperors were created and deposed in rapid succession, she ascended the Throne herself in 593 A. D. Umako became the Prime Minister, while her own nephew, the celebrated Shotoku Taishi, was appointed Heir Apparent. The latter was at the same time appointed the Regent of the realm, the Empress probably thinking it proper, in view of want of precedence for placing the crown upon a woman's head, to abstain from a direct share in the government of the country. At all events, she was happy in her choice of the Regent, for under his wise and benevolent administration the country enjoyed a long and unbroken peace, the results of which were discernible in the increasing prosperity of the people and in the striding progress they made in politics, industry, literature and the arts. It was during this period that students and priests were first sent to China to study her civilization and introduce here whatever was good and excellent in it. This wise Crown Prince died earlier than the Empress.

The next female sovereign was the Empress Kokyoku, who ascended the Throne in 642 A. D. She had been the consort of the Emperor Kimmei. She had borne a son to him, but the Prince was still too young to be crowned, and consequently she herself became the Empress. In administration she had the advantage of the wise counsel of her son, Nakano Oye, and her Prime Minister, Kamatari, the founder of the noble house of Fujiwara, and one of the greatest statesmen that ever ruled Japan. By the advice of these remarkable men the Empress continued and brought nearer to completion the great work of political and social renovation, which had been begun under the reign of the Empress Suiko. She abdicated the Throne in favor of her younger brother, but upon his demise her son, Naka no Oye, still declining to accept the Crown, she again assumed the Imperial powers. For her second reign she is known by the title of Saimei Tenno. In the reign of the Empress Saimei, Corea was invaded by China and troops were dispatched to the peninsula to protect the State of Kudara, which then acknowledged Japan's authority, against the Chinese invaders. The Empress, accompanied by Prince Naka no Oye, went as far as Kyushu, where, unfortunately, she was overtaken by the most dreadful enemy—death.

The next female ruler was the Empress Jito, who ascended the Throne in A. D. 690. A daughter of the Emperor Tenchi, she was the consort of the Emperor Temmu, after whose demise, and until she assumed the Imperial title, she actually exercised the Imperial functions for several years.

She soon left the Throne in favor of one of her grandsons, but her successor being under age, she still continued the virtual ruler of the Empire. Upon the death of the Emperor Mombu, as her successor has since been named, she once more accepted the Crown and was known as the Empress Gemmei. It was during the reign of this Empress that the Capital of the country was removed to Nara in 708 A. D.

In 715 she was succeeded by her daughter, who is known in history as the Empress Gensho. She held the Crown for only nine years.

The next female occupant of the Throne was the Empress Koken, a daughter of the Emperor Shomu. She assumed regal powers in 749 A. D. She abdicated the Crown in favor of the Crown Prince, who has since been given the posthumous name of the Emperor Junnin. A difference arising between him and the ex-Empress, the latter deposed him and again assumed the Imperial title. For her second reign she is known by the name of the Empress Koya. The Empress was a woman of remarkable character and gave proofs of extraordinary aptitude for administration. But the latter years of her reign were disgraced by her excessive partiality to Buddhist priests, who filled every post of trust and importance at Court. There was even danger of the Crown being placed upon the head of a priest, a disgrace from which the country was happily saved by the courage and tact of that loyalist, Wakeno Kiyomaro.

The unfortunate experience of her reign taught the country that it was undesirable to have a woman upon the Throne, and for about ten centuries following it was exclusively occupied by men.

In 1630 the Throne was again graced by a woman, the Empress Meisho. In 1763 there was another Empress, called Gosakuramachi. These two Empresses held the Crown when the actual powers of government were in the hands of the Shogunate, and they had, consequently, little scope for the exercise of their capacity.

It will be seen from the above sketch that, with the exception of the two last mentioned Empresses, all the rest reigned between the sixth and the eighth centuries. With the exception of the Empress Koken, they do not seem to have personally attended to State affairs. It must not, however, be inferred from this that they did not exercise any political influence. On the contrary, many of them wielded considerable political as well as social influence. Especially is this true of the Empresses Suiko, Kokyoku, Jito and Koken, during whose reigns the country made steady and remarkable progress in politics, religion, literature and the arts. Their proficiency in literature is amply proved by specimens of their poems preserved in classical collections.

## Imperial Consorts.

Since the eighth century, there have been only two female sovereigns; but there have been not a few Imperial Consorts who are entitled to honorable mention in history. Especially was this the case during the so-called Age of Nara (710–793 A. D.). It was during this period that women of culture and talent exercised vast influence in the refined society of the Capital. Of all the Imperial Consorts during this period none deserve our attention more than the Consort of the Emperor Shomu, who was called Komyo Kogo (Empress of Glory), on account of the brilliancy and beauty of her countenance. She was a daughter of Fujiwara no Fuhito, one of the remarkable statesmen of the age. She was married to the Emperor Shomu in her sixteenth year and while he was still Heir Apparent. She was of a very charitable disposition, and a devoted believer in Buddhism. It was by her advice that the Emperor Shomu caused the construction of the Todaiji temple at Nara, of which the great bronze statue of Buddha is now the wonder and admiration of visitors from every clime of the world. What was, perhaps, even more remarkable for that age was the establishment by her of asylums and free hospitals for the poor. She was very skilled in penmanship, which is regarded in Japan almost in the light of a fine art, and was noted for proficiency in prose composition. After the death of her Imperial spouse, she displayed remarkable aptitude for administrative work as guardian for the Empress Koken.

The Imperial Consort of the Emperor Saga, named Kachi Ko, was a daughter of Tachibana Kiyotomo, a court noble. She was of very calm and gentle temper, while her countenance is said to have been uncommonly pretty. Her virtues were such that, under the beneficial influence of her example, perfect harmony and peace reigned among the numerous inmates of the Court. She was loved as well as respected by the Emperor. She, like the rest of Empresses, was a pious believer in Buddhism, and constructed a temple called Danrin-ji. She also interested herself in educational affairs and established a college for the education of the youths of the family of Tachibana. When her son, the Emperor Ninmei, was seriously ill she grieved so much that it visibly injured her health. She finally became a nun and died at the age of 65.

Among the numerous children of the Imperial Consort just mentioned, Princess Masa Ko was most remarkable for intelligence and beauty. She became the Empress of the Emperor Junna. She rendered valuable services to her husband by giving him wise counsels in matters of government. On one occasion she went out to see the farmers at work in the fields and encouraged them by giving them valuable gifts with her own hands. Upon the death of her husband she shaved her head and became a nun. She devoted the remainder of her years to various charitable works, among which may be mentioned the establishment of a free hospital for priests in the compounds of the Daikakuji, which was also erected by her.

The Imperial Consort of the Emperor Murakami, named Yasuko, was a daughter of Fujiwara Morosuke, Minister of the Right. She was distinguished for the sincerity of her friendship. She is said to have been of inestimable assistance to her husband as his political adviser. Whatever advice she gave it was at once adopted by the Emperor. Unfortunately, she died quite young, lamented by men and women of every class.

The Consort of the Emperor Yen-Yu (970-985 A. D.), was the daughter of Fujiwara no Kaneiye. When her son, the Emperor Ichijo, succeeded to the Throne, she administered the Government during his minority. Even after he attained manhood he generally followed the advice of his experienced and accomplished mother. She, like many of her predecessors, built several Buddhist temples, of which the Jitokuji and the Gedatsuji may be mentioned. She died at the early age of 40.

The Consort of the Emperor Ichijo (987-1011 A. D.), named Aki ko, was a daughter of Fujiwara no Michinaga. She was not only uncommonly beautiful in person but well versed in Japanese and Chinese literatures. Among her maids of honor there were several talented ladies who have immortalized their names as the pioneers of *belles-lettres* in Japan; the most distinguished among them being Murasaki-shikibu, the graceful authoress of the " *Genji Monogatari.*" Besides her literary accomplishments she was universally loved and respected for her singular freedom from the petty vices of temper to which her sex is peculiarly liable. In her old age she became a nun and devoted herself to the services of religion. She built the temple of Tohoku-in. She lived to the venerable age of 87.

There were other Imperial Consorts who have left their marks on the political history of the country, but want of space compels us to omit them from the list. The age in which the graceful Consort of the Emperor Ichijo lived, marked the most prosperous period of the Imperial Court in ancient times. Henceforth the powers of State rapidly drifted into the hands of the military class, and with the political power all the glory and accomplishments hitherto gathered together about the Court in Kyoto, utterly disappeared.

### The Age of Kamakura.

It is, perhaps, well that we should describe more fully the transfer of power from the Court to the military class alluded to, at the end of the preceding chapter. To speak more exactly, the transfer of power was not from the Court, but from the House of Fujiwara to the military class. For two centuries, from the middle of the ninth to the middle of the eleventh, the sons of the Fujiwara House, as hereditary Ministers of the Crown, exercised absolute sway at Court. They made and unmade Emperors just as it suited their convenience or their whims. All the marks of honor and official ambition were monopolized by the numerous members of the dominant family. Their long continued monopoly of power and their increasing luxury and extravagance had, on the one hand, the effect of sapping their vitality and converting them into a set of impotent and helpless dotards, and, on the other, finally brought upon their heads the dreadful vengeance of the class, which they had systematically oppressed for 200 years, and which had been during that period gradually nursing its power to strike a death blow at its arrogant oppressors. The first military family to rise to power as successor to the House of Fujiwara was the Taira or Heike, as it is more popularly called. The Heike in its turn was supplanted by another military family, the Minamoto or Genji. With the victory of Yoritomo, the leader of the Genji family, over the Heike, and with the establishment of his Shogunate Government at Kamakura, dates the completion of the feudal system, which, with occasional modifications, remained in force for seven centuries, until the Restoration in 1868. This long period of time will be divided for the purposes of the present work into the Age of Kamakura, the Age of Ashikaga, and the Age of Tokugawa.

The Age of Kamakura covers an interval of about 130 years from the establishment of the Shogunate Government at Kamakura to the fall of the family at Hojo. Under the benign and economical administration of the Kamakura Shoguns and their ministers, the country enjoyed the benefits of peace and prosperity. Among the several remarkable women who appeared on the political stage during this age the foremost place must be given to Masa ko, the wife of Yoritomo.

### Taira No Masako.

Taira no Masako was the eldest daughter of Hojo Tokimasa, a military officer of some importance belonging to the Heike and living in the Province of Izu. Her mother having died in her infancy, she was taken care of by a step-mother, who had also a daughter. There lived in the neighborhood of Masako's house a young prisoner of State, at large under the surveillance of her father. This was Yoritomo, whose father had been defeated in a futile attempt to bring about the downfall of the Heike in 1158. Yoritomo was originally placed under the joint custody of Ito Sukechika and Hojo Tokimasa. There arose some trouble between Ito and Yoritomo, and the latter was afterward taken care of principally by Hojo Tokimasa.

Hearing that Tokimasa had daughters, Yoritomo was desirous of obtaining the hand of one. With this object in view, he asked information about each of them. He was told that the elder, who was by the former wife of Tokimasa, was 21 years of age and very pretty, and that the younger, real daughter of the present wife was 19, and inferior to her sister in point of beauty. Being a wary young man, Yoritomo thought it wiser to apply for the hand of the younger daughter, so as to please the wife of his custodian. He wrote a letter to the younger daughter presenting himself as a suitor, and entrusted its delivery to a man enjoying his confidence. This individual, thinking that, as the girl in question being otherwise than pretty, the match would not be a happy one, took it upon himself to destroy the letter, and, writing a new one in Yoritomo's name, secretly delivered it to the elder daughter. Masako was overjoyed with the proposal, for she said she had a dream the previous night which indicated Yoritomo as her future husband.

Masatoki happened at the time to be away on duty in the Capital. At the expiration of his term of service, he came home in the company of Taira no Kanetaka, who was Lieutenant-Governor of the Province. Tokimasa was naturally desirous of establishing himself in high favor with this distinguished dignitary. He consequently promised to give him his eldest daughter in marriage. We may easily imagine his surprise and embarrassment when he was told on getting home that Masako had plighted her faith to Yoritomo. He was well aware that Yoritomo was no ordinary man, but that he was destined to leave his mark in history. He would therefore have been but too glad to give his daughter to him, had he not given his word of honor to Kanetaka. So, appearing not to know anything about what had passed between Masako and Yoritomo, the worthy father sent his daughter to Kanetaka. But on the night of the wedding, when rain was pouring down heavily, the bride, secretly escaping from the bridegroom's house, took refuge in a neighboring mountain, and managed somehow to acquaint Yoritomo with her hiding place. Yoritomo soon joined his faithful lover there, where they lived together for some time. The disappointed bridegroom instituted searches for his missing wife, but no trace of her could be discovered. Tokimasa, on the other hand, showed no concern about his daughter's mysterious disappearance.

Meanwhile the growing impudence and brutal despotism of the Heike, or House of Taira, had driven Prince Mochihito to take desperate measures for the suppression of that family. To that end he issued summons to the remnants of the Genji, or the House of Minamoto. Yoritomo was, of course, one of the principal recipients of the summons. He, in concert with his father-in-law, raised his standard at Mount Ishibashi in the Province of Izu. The remarkable series of events, which finally ended in the establishment of Yoritomo as the actual ruler of the country, are entirely beyond the scope of the present work. Suffice it to say, that the first of the Shoguns owed his extraordinary success, in no small degree, to the valuable assistance and unfailing exhortation of his remarkable wife.

Masako was, above all things, distinguished for the masculine character of her mind and heart; and it is recorded that even her strong-willed husband was in fear of her. At one time Yoritomo took his eldest son on a hunting excursion in the plains at the base of Fujisan, when the latter shot a deer. Overjoyed at the prowess shown by his son, Yoritomo at once despatched a special messenger to his wife to inform her of the joyful event. The messenger was astonished to find his mistress genuinely displeased with the fuss her husband made over such a trifling affair. "Was there anything," she asked, "worthy of particular applause in the son of the Shogun shooting a deer?" Upon the death of Yoritomo, Masako shaved her head and assumed the habit of a nun, but from that time she became the real center of power, for the succeeding Shoguns were all men of inferior capacity. Yoriiye, for instance, paid no attention to administrative affairs, being addicted to debauchery of the most offensive type. At one time he was in imminent danger of losing his life by an insult offered to a mistress of one of his generals. In other respects, also, he made himself hateful to his officers, and had it not been for the assiduous admonitions and untiring address of his mother, his house would have been early subverted by one of his own generals. His dissipation and neglect of duties growing more and more intolerable, Masako, after consulting her father, Tokimasa, compelled him to resign the office of Shogun. Masako wanted to divide the country into two parts, and give the control of one portion to Ichiman, son of Yoriiye, and the other half to Sanetomo, his (Yoriiye's) younger brother. Yoriiye's father-in-law, Hiki Yoshikazu, who had been indignant at his son-in-law's deposition, greatly objected to see one-half of the rightful heritage taken away from his grandson. He resolved, together with Yoriiye, to assassinate Masako and her father Tokimasa. But this conspiracy was discovered by Masako. Hiki Yoshikazu and his family, as well as Ichiman, were all beheaded; while Yoriiye was confined at the Shuzenji in Izu. The Shogunate title was given to Sanetomo.

In 1218, Masako visited the temples at Kumano in the Province of Kishu. On her way back, she visited Kyoto, where the Emperor Gotoba conferred upon her the rank of the second grade of the third class. The Emperor expressed a wish to give an audience to her, but she declined it, saying that a rustic old woman was not fit to appear before such an august person. Her rank was soon after raised to the second class, and so she is very often known by the name of *Ni-i no Ama* (a nun of the rank of the second class).

Sanetomo was assassinated by Kugyo, a son of Yoriiye. With him expired all the descendants of Yoritomo, and the fortune of the house was at its lowest point. There were several revolts, but they were promptly put down by her resolution and courage. There being no heir to the Shogunate office, she applied to the Emperor for permission to adopt one of the princes as heir; but this application having been refused, she again applied and received permission to place Yoritsune, a two-year-old child of a court noble, Fujiwara no Michiiye, in the office of Shogun. Masako, as before, exercised the real power of government as the guardian of the Shogun.

In the period of Jokyu (1219–1221) an attempt was made by the Imperialist party at Kyoto to overturn the Shogunate government at Kamakura. Its failure was due to the promptitude and decision shown by the aged guardian of the Shogun. On the first report of unusual movements in Kyoto,

Masako called together the generals, who had fought under her deceased husband, and caused one of her officers, Adachi Kagemori, to address them in a manner appealing with peculiar force to their sense of honor and their personal gratitude to their late master. They all vowed their unfailing attachment to the cause of the Shogunate. Masako, we read in history, took the leading part in the council of war held at her father's house on the eve of despatching troops to Kyoto.

She was conspicuous for cool courage. At one time, after the death of the Regent Yoshitoki, and while his successor was still unsettled, his second wife organized a conspiracy to have her son elected to the office, to the exclusion of Yasutoki, her stepson, who in the natural order of things ought to receive the appointment. Masako taking only a maid with her, called on Miura Yoshimura, one of the conspirators, in the dead of night, and rebuked him for his conduct. He confessed all, and repented of what he had done. The conspiracy was thus nipped in the bud.

She died in 1225, at the age of 69.

## The Age of Ashikaga.

The best portion of the so-called Age of Kamakura was really the age of Hojo, because the Hojo, as hereditary Regents of the Shogun, exercised the real powers of the government. There were eight generations of such Regents. They were able to maintain their power so long, first, because they showed unceasing concern for the true welfare of the people; and secondly, because they took care to excite as little envy and jealousy as possible by adhering to an unaffected and frugal style of living. There is an interesting story, well illustrating the secret of power possessed by the House of Hojo. Matsushita Zen-ni, at one time invited to her house her son, Tokiyori, who was then Regent in the Shogunate. Among other preparations for receiving her son, Matsushita Zen-ni mended the *shoji* (paper screen) by pasting over the ragged holes with pieces of paper, when her brother, Adachi Yasumori, happened to come to the house. He advised her to renew the paper entirely. She, however, quietly told her brother that her object in making patch-work repairs was to illustrate before her sons the truth "That injuries mended before they become serious save much time and labor."

The eighth Regent, Takatoki, unlike his predecessors, was arrogant in temper and extravagant in life. With him ended the Shogunate government at Kamakura.

The next house of Shogun was called Ashikaga. During the period of transition between the new and old order of things, there were two women, who deserve an honorable place in these pages. One was the wife of that great loyalist, Kusunoki Masashige. Unfortunately, the knowledge we possess of her is excessively scanty. But there can be no doubt that she was a woman of remarkable character. When her husband, Masashige, fell in battle, his antagonist, Ashikaga, generously sent his head to her—a favor rarely granted in those troublous times. Her son, Masatsura, a boy of 11, was so overwhelmed with sorrow that he attempted to commit suicide. His mother strongly rebuked him for his rashness and brought him up a worthy successor to his immortal father.

The other lady was the mother of another loyalist, Uryu Tamotsu. He raised the Imperial standard in the Province of Echizen with Wakiya Yoshiharu as his chief. He was, however, beaten by his enemy and fell fighting hand to hand, surrounded by most of his fellow generals. When the disastrous news reached his castle, where his chief Wakiya was staying, it threw the inmates into a frenzy of lamentation. His mother alone was able to control her strong feelings. She quietly came forward to the presence of Wakiya and said "That she was glad that her son had fallen in war in company with such distinguished generals." She pointed to three of her sons still remaining alive and bade her chief Wakiya be of good cheer so long as her sons were still alive. Her heroic fortitude acted like a charm, and it is said that the drooping spirits of the party instantly revived with redoubled energy. Instances of such heroism on the part of women were numerous in those warlike times.

These ladies lived in the middle of the fourteenth century. After that time the House of the Ashikaga exercised the Shogunate authority for about a century. From the middle of the fifteenth century, the Ashikaga Shogunate began to lose its power until it was finally supplanted by Oda Nobunaga, who was succeeded by Toyotomi Hideyoshi, one of the most remarkable men produced in Japan.

His wife was an extraordinary woman. He, no doubt, in a measure, owed his great success in life to the assistance and inspiration he received from her. She was a daughter of Asano Matazayemon, a native of Owari. Mayeda Toshiiye, the founder of the noble family of Mayeda of Kaga, paid court to her, and her father strongly advised her to return his affection, but she rejected his offer, and accepted that of Toki-chiro, an inferior officer in the household of Nobunaga. It is stated that, being extremely poor, they celebrated their nuptial ceremony by sitting on a straw mat and using a broken earthenware vessel as a wine cup. After Tokichiro became the ruler of the country he was reminded by his wife of the occasion of their marriage whenever he showed a tendency to fall into an extravagant way of living. She was not only intelligent, but particularly remarkable for her virtuous character. Had she lived longer, it is believed, that the House of Toyotomi would not have fallen so soon, but in fact she survived her husband only a short time.

To those illustrious names we must in justice add that of Yamanouchi Chiyo Ko, whose prudence, courage and wisdom are widely known to have been highly instrumental to her husband's unequaled promotion.

## Lady Yamanouchi Chiyo Ko.

Lady Yamanouchi Chiyo Ko, wife of Yamanouchi Kazu-toyo, the Lord of Tosa, was the daughter of Wakamiya Tomooki, vassal of Lord Arai of Omi. When she was yet an infant her father died in an unknown battle leaving no heir to his estate. This sad bereavement caused her and her mother to find their home with the husband of one of her aunts, and when 18 she was married to Lord Yamanou-chi. Possessed of a keen wit, an elevated spirit, a lively fancy, and a strong sense of moral purity, she was equal to every household duty, so that her husband could devote all his energies to political and military matters. Nor was this all. She gave such wise counsel and spirited assistance to her husband on many important occasions, that we doubt whether

he could have risen to that height of fame and fortune, had he
not been so fortunate in his marriage.

When she married, her husband was living in a very
small way, and she had to put up with all the privations in-
cident to poverty. This, however, weighed but little upon
her brave heart. She played so well her part of home mana-
ger that Kazutoyo thought of nothing but to find a worthy
master, whom he fortunately found in Oda Nobunaga.
While his master was at the Adzuchi castle, a jockey appeared
with a superb charger. Many of Nobunaga's retainers wanted
to buy it, but the price asked was too much for them to afford.
Kazutoyo, too, desired to have it, but knowing its price too
great for his embarrassed condition went home to his bride.
Chiyo Ko observed Kazutoyo's unusual thoughtfulness and
asked him the reason. He told her all about the charger, and
said, "If I should appear before my new master upon such an
animal, I cannot but gain his admiration. How painful that
it is too expensive for me to buy." So saying, he shed a flood
of tears and bitterly regretted that his poverty should make
him lose so rare an opportunity of gaining his master's good
graces. Hereupon Chiyo Ko asked what the price of the
horse was, and being told that it was ten *rio*, she surprised
her husband thus: "If no more than that, you can have the
animal. I have the money." She forthwith produced the
sum from a case in which she used to keep her mirror.
Kazutoyo was extremely astonished and said: "What an
iron-heart yours is not to have produced this gold before?
Have we not often come to the verge of starvation?" "What
you say," replied Chiyo Ko, "is simply reasonable. My
mother placed this sum in my mirror case on the eve of my
espousals, with strict injunction not to spend it, till a matter
of great consequence on your part required it. Poverty have
I borne with little pain, as it is no uncommon fate to be of
straitened means in such a warlike age as this." Kazutoyo
was then rejoiced beyond all description, and immediately
made the horse his own and held it no less dear than his wife.
A little while after it chanced that Nobunaga inspected his
retainers' horses, when the charger in question caught the
great general's eye. He demanded who its owner was.
Hereupon Kazutoyo spoke about its purchase, excepting the

part his wife had had in it. Then the general lavished a
series of eulogiums upon the lucky soldier, and said: "The
jockey must have brought the horse here thinking no other
clansmen would be able to buy it. And so, had it not been for
you, an irrevocable disgrace must have fallen upon our house.
That you, who have been so long out of employment, could
afford to strike the bargain, shows you no ordinary man. You
deserve ever so large an addition to your pay." This paved,
as the reader knows, his way to all future elevation.

After the unnatural death of Nobunaga, Kazutoyo went
to serve the famous Hideyoshi. In 1600 Tokugawa Iyeyasu
and Hidetada went to the north to subdue Uyesugi Kagekatsu.
Kazutoyo had gone with them, leaving his wife in Osaka.
When Iyeyasu was at Oyama, in the Province of Shimotzuke
and Kazutoyo in Morokawa, not far from the future Shogun's
camp, a faint rumor reached their ears that Ishida Kazushige,
more popularly known as Ishida Mitsunari, a favorite of Hideyoshi's, was going to take them by surprise from the rear, in
order to slay Iyeyasu and his son. This rumor turned out an
actual event known in history as the battle of Sekigahara.
While yet Iyeyasu was entertaining doubts as to the truth of
the report, a messenger came to Kazutoyo from his wife. He
brought a letter-box and a paper cap-string, which bore all
the signs of its having been attached to the messenger's cap
all the way down from Osaka. The future Lord of Tosa un-
rolled the string, and who can imagine his astonishment, when
he saw written therein all the complex intrigues of Mitsunari's, and the earnest advice to unite his interests to
those of Tokugawa. Kazutoyo ran to Oyama, though
it was long after dusk, told Iyeyasu the contents of
his wife's string-epistle, and gave him the letter-box
unopened. They uncovered the box together and found in it
a long letter, in Chiyo Ko's own handwriting, fully stating all
they wanted to know about Osaka. This information, especially the string-letter, did much to enable Iyeyasu to win the
battle of Sekigahara. It was, indeed, mainly in view of this
valuable news that Kazutoyo was created the Lord of Tosa
with an estate worth 230,000 *koku* of rice per year, after
Iyeyasu came to rule the whole country. Had not Chiyoko
resorted to the said device of making the more important

letter into a string to be worn on her messenger's cap, while putting the less important one in a letter-box, so that its conveyance seemed the only errand the bearer had, it would never have reached its destination. What a stretch of ingenuity!

During the battle of Sekigahara the wives and children of all the warriors who had gone north under Iyeyasu were to be confined as hostages in the Osaka castle. After this was decided upon, officers were first sent to the wife of Hosokawa Tadaoki, the Lord of Ettchiu, to inform her that she and her children must present themselves at the castle to be therein detained as hostages. Then the spirited lady killed her two children, burned her house and finally slew herself. This news reached the ears of our heroine and she determined to follow Lady Hosokawa's brave example. Chiyo Ko told her desperate intention to an old man named Yamashiro who had been sent to her from Morokawa and her husband as household adviser, and requested him to behead her after she opened her abdomen like a brave soldier. Yamashiro prevailed upon her to delay her self-destruction, until he ascertained whether or not the tide of things had turned. The old man went about the town after the desired information, but he found the gates, within which he had hoped to pass, all shut, both upon him and any other visitor. He then made use of an arrow as a messenger to a neighbor who sent his reply by the same inanimate bearer, to the effect that the hostage question in the form first decided on was abandoned on account of its having caused so appalling a disaster to Lady Hosokawa. Thus was Chiyo Ko disuaded from dying.

Shortly afterward Chiyo Ko, as well as all the other noble wives whose husbands had gone to the north under Iyeyasu, was ordered to send any one of her relatives to the castle as hostage. Thereupon she sent Niwo, a nephew of Kazutoyo, into the fortress together with two brave attendants. Niwo was returned to her safe and sound at the restoration of peace and order.

Chiyo Ko bore a daughter in 1585. The child was named Yonehime, was loved extremely by both its parents until it grew to be 6 years of age, when its father's castle was shaken to the ground by an earthquake and it was crushed to death under a falling beam. A few days after the catastrophe, while Chiyo Ko had yet her eyes bedewed with the tears of lamentation, one of her favorite maids brought her news that a foundling, supposed to be a warrior's son from its being possessed of a sword, had been found near one end of the castle town. She forthwith had the poor boy brought to her mansion, and bade her servants nurture him as her son, thinking that she had obtained a suitable person by asking a priest to pray for the repose of Yonehime's soul. Kazutoyo saw the child growing more and more lovable and often showed a desire to make him his heir. Seeing this, Chiyo Ko was grieved to her heart's very core, but feeling that a fruitful seed of misery was about to be sown, she sent him away to a great Buddhist patriarch, Nankwa Kokushi by name; telling him the mission she had destined him to fulfill, and giving him a purse heavy with gold. After the boy was thus in priests' orders, Kazutoyo adopted Tadayoshi, one of his nephews, as his son and successor.

Strong-hearted and manly as she was, she did not the less value petty feminine industries like penmanship and sewing. While in the Nagahama castle she prepared a beautiful gown by stitching together small pieces of many varieties of cloths so skillfully that it found its way into the Imperial wardrobe through the admiring persuasion of her husband's dear friends and that of the Prime Minister of the Crown.

This great woman must be esteemed as having possessed all the four female virtues of Confucius, of which we have given a brief account in the introductory chapter. After her husband's death she removed to a convent, which she had erected in Kyoto, and then led the pure life of a nun, dedicating herself wholly to Kazutoyo's and Yonehime's memory until her peaceful death, which took place in 1617, when she was 61 years of age. The reason for which she went to Kyoto after Kazutoyo's death is twofold: First, to see the great teacher, Nankwa Kokushi, and to hear from him the great doctrines of Buddha; and secondly, to enjoy the society of the foundling she had so carefully educated and who had then become a great priest as Shonan Osho.

## The Age of Tokugawa.

After the battle of Sekigahara, Iyeyasu, the winner, made all the turbulent chiefs pay homage to him. He was a statesman with uncommonly developed common sense, and a rare gift of nature for command. He laid down a series of rules, widely known as the first Shogun's Instructions, to be strictly observed by all his successors, whose observance of them was proverbially strict.

The House of Tokugawa ruled the country for 270 years, represented by fifteen Shoguns. At its height of power and splendor it seemed as if destined to rule the country forever. But true to the nature of all false things it was merely "An apple fine to look at, but rotten at the core." Toward the end of the eighteenth century it commenced to show signs of decay. Commodore Perry and other national representatives soon appeared in the seas and made the national burden too heavy to be borne by the effeminate progeny of the great Iyeyasu. And the memorable year 1868 saw the powers of the State restored to the Crown, after over seven hundred years since they had been usurped from the Imperial hand.

During the Tokugawa age women were generally kept down, and none of their sex made their names very illustrious, as the whole country was kept in order as if by a myriad of little mechanical contrivances strictly in obedience to Iyeyasu's careful instructions, and it was greatly and reasonably feared that female influence, which has been marvelously powerful in all ages and places, might dash the whole nicely balanced structure into pieces. But nature was stronger, as she always is, than man, and we hear of some women who lived in this age, fully worthy of brief mention here.

## Ocha no Tsubone.

She was the daughter of Iida Kiuzaemon, of the Takeda clan of Kai. She was married to Kano Magobei, of the Imagawa clan. It fell to her and Magobei's lot to administer to the comforts and conveniences of Iyeyasu, when the latter was once detained in their master's castle as hostage. When afterward her husband died a soldier's death in the same battle in which his master, Imagawa Yoshimoto, fought and died, she returned to Kai and lived with her brother, Inosuke. The Takeda clan was subjugated soon after her return to Kai; to wit, it met with the same fate as the one to which her husband had belonged.

One day after she had become poverty stricken, she made bold to stop Iyeyasu, who was then in Kai on some important business, upon a road, and to tell him about her eventful life. Iyeyasu was moved to tears, took her back to his castle and created her his chief maid.

After that she went many a time to the Osaka castle, when peace negotiations were going on between the Tokugawa and Toyotomi houses, and contributed not a little toward their satisfactory conclusion.

When the daughter of the second Shogun, Hidetada, was married to the Emperor Go-Mizuwo, she was appointed to the highly honorable nuptial office of representing the bride's mother at Court, and so pleased the Emperor that he conferred upon her the rank of the second grade of the first class. It is extremely to be regretted that no more of her career, which, if known more minutely would be highly interesting and instructive, is handed down to us.

### Kasuga no Tsubone.

This lady was a nurse to Iyemitsu, the third of the Tokugawa line. She was a daughter of Saito Rizo, one of Akechi's retainers, and wife of Inaba Masashige, the Lord of Sado. She had three sons, respectively named Masakatsu, Masasada and Masatoshi. Her husband, a subject of Ukita Hideiye, did not seek a new master after the Osaka castle, and with it his master had fallen. He confined himself in his native town to spend his remaining days in honorable obscurity, when Takechiyo, afterward the third Shogun Iyemitsu, was born, and his wife was appointed his nurse. As years went by it was painfully felt by her that Kunimatsu, the younger brother of her protégé, was more beloved by their mother; that most people respected the younger more than the elder, and that therefore the former's influence was far more powerful than the latter's. She thought this no light matter. She visited Iyeyasu, who was then in Shizuoka bearing the title of Ogosho or 'retired Shogun,' on her way to the Imperial shrines in Ise, and told him all that weighed so heavily upon her loyal heart. The ex-Shogun was greatly astonished and soon after made a visit to the Edo castle. Then the reigning Shogun, who was noted for the sincerity of his filial piety, gave a grand feast to his father. In it Iyeyasu gave Takechiyo the honor of sitting close to him, while ordering Kunimatsu to sit an apartment away, thus intimating to all present whom he meant for the third of his line. From this day upward Takechiyo's influence became equal to that of the heir apparent to the Shogunate. It is needless to say how much Takechiyo owed this elevation to his nurse.

Upon Takechiyo's taking the power of the Shogunate, Kasuga was entrusted with the management of all matters concerning the interior chambers of his palace.

Once she went to Kyoto on duty and was then made the recipient of the great honor of being called into the Imperial presence. Kasuga, a name by which she is best known in history, was given her by the Emperor on that occasion. It means *vernal day*. The Empress gave her a wine cup with her own hand.

Kasuga died a happy death in September, 1643, after a short illness. When the Shogun heard that she was dangerously sick, he administered to her a medicine of his own preparation, and enjoined her to ask her last favor of him. The dying nurse expressed her thanks quite intelligibly, but said nothing more. Then Iyemitsu said: "If you have nothing to ask on your part, let me tell you that I have something on mine. It is this: pardon your youngest son Masatoshi. I have not yet had the pleasure of seeing him, as he has been under your sentence of *kando* since I was a mere boy (*kando* or *kanki* was a custom of turning a disobedient son out of a family by way of punishment). I and he have sucked the same breast and I cannot but feel a sort of brotherly sympathy towards him. Will you, therefore, pardon him for my sake, if not for his?" "I abandoned him," replied Kasuga, who was about to breathe her last, "as I had seen in him a bad disposition, which is sure to lead him away from the path of dutiful obedience to your highness, much to the disadvantage of the Shogunate government. Be kind enough not to make me forget the faithful servant in the fond mother. Do not, please, pardon him even after my death for the repose of my departed soul." The moment she uttered the last word, she was no more.

The House of Tokugawa had many another worthy maid, whom we should be only too glad to introduce to the reader, if our space was equal to our wishes.

Toward the close of the Tokugawa period many worthy women appeared embracing the Emperor's cause. We can, however, find no more space here than to give a brief sketch of one of them.

### Muraoka Tsubone.

She was the daughter of Tsuzaki Motonori, one of the domestics of Prince Daikakuji. She was born near Saga in 1786, and died in August, 1873, at the venerable age of 88. When 8 years of age she entered the household of Prince Konoye as a maid. As she grew up, her talents and courage raised her to the rank of *Rojo* (literally rendered, *old woman*) or chief maid to her master, the Minister of the Left. The age she lived in, when the Shogunate government was at its lowest ebb of prosperity, was peculiarly fitted to satisfy her passion for loyal service. She served as a sort of go-between to several great Imperialists of her time, such as Saigo Takamori, the Priest Gessho, and her own master. Her part of the patriotic service was, in her age, simply indispensable, as it was next to impossible for one of the *samurai* class to get an interview with anyone of royal blood. She was always prepared to risk her life, if for the sake of the Emperor. She was once taken before the Shogun's judges on charge of treason, and upon trial sentenced to a three months' imprisonment. The part she played as a woman having free access to the close relatives of the Emperor, to high court officials, and to the Imperialists of the *samurai* and *heimin* classes was inestimably valuable.

After the Restoration she built a convent called Chokushi-an in Saga, where the great Saigo often visited her to enjoy repeating the tales about things past; and not seldom to shed joyful tears to the memory of the dangers they had experienced. In 1872 the Emperor was pleased to fix upon her a life pension of twenty *koku* of rice per year, and to raise her memory to the rank of the second grade of the fourth class in the last year but one. She generously gave to the poor all that she could save of the Imperial endowment.

We shall make here no mention of the worthy members of our sex, who have appeared since the Revolution of 1868. In conformity to the valuable precept alluded to in the opening lines of this chapter, the womanly virtues have been, and are mostly destined not to shine before the public eye. So the reader can rest assured that those who have been mentioned above were women of the very first rank in merit: Other gems of less luster must have been buried in oblivion.

In conclusion let us give the valuable words of Fujiwara no Yoshimoto, who lived some four hundred years ago:

"Women must obey their parents when young, must obey their husbands in the best years of their lives, and must obey their children when aged. Theirs it is to be meek and harmonious with all they have to deal with. But since this country is named *Wakoku*, or the Country of Harmony, it may be her doom to be governed by the fair sex. Was not the great Tensho Taijin a woman? Of what sex was Jingo Kogo, who conquered Corea and made her acknowledge our country's authority over her? Was it not the wife of Yoritomo, who actually ruled the country for many a year after her illustrious husband's death? Do we not hear of not a few Empresses holding the reins of government quite creditably in the days of old? May we not very likely be placed under a great Empress in no distant future?"

# CHAPTER III.

## JAPANESE WOMEN IN LITERATURE.

---

### INTRODUCTION.

In early Japan there were no letters or ideographs. It was in 284 A. D., i. e., nearly a thousand years after the foundation of the Empire by Jimmu Tenno when the Corean scholar, Wani, came over to this land of the Rising Sun and instructed her sons in the Chinese characters and literature, so that she then first heard of the existence of written language. It was, however, quite common among our unlettered ancestors to chant what was pleasing or surprising to their eyes or ears, in a form of metrical language called *uta*, the rhythm of whose lines were well calculated to please the ear and to help the memory. The *uta* or poem was, as it is now, of two varieties as regards its length—the longer *uta*, or *Choka*, and the shorter, or *Tanka;* the former consisting of an indefinite number of feet, of which some are of five and others of seven syllables, and the latter of thirty-one syllables, i. e., of two five-syllabled, and three seven-syllabled feet:   Here are examples.

### A Longer *Uta* (*Choka*).

| | |
|---|---|
| Yasumishishi | Waga Ohokimi no |
| Ashita ni wa | Torinadetamahi |
| Yufube ni wa | Iyosetateteshi |
| Mitoraji no | Adzusa no yumi no |
| Nagahazu no | Otosu nari |
| Asakari ni | Imatatasurashi |
| Mitoraji no | Adzusa no yumi no |
| Nagahazu no | Otosu nari |

### A Shorter *Uta* (*Tanka*).

| | |
|---|---|
| Tamakiharu | Uchino ohnu ni |
| Umanamete | Asafumasuran |
| Sonokusafukenu | |

39

At the present time the longer variety is very seldom composed, and the word *uta* has come to be nearly synonymous with *tanka*. Besides the two varieties above mentioned some modifications of them once used to be composed, which differed from their originals only in containing a few syllables more or less. They are only used now on particular occasions.

Of the *uta* belonging to the period preceding the use of letters only a few remain, but quite a number exist of those composed between the introduction of Chinese ideographs and the invention of *Kana*. Some of those ancient poems are highly heroic, like unto a warrior on horseback about to discharge an arrow from a doubled bow; some very soft and sweet, like unto beautiful maidens sitting under flower-laden boughs, dressed in robes of silk brocade; and others extremely sorrowful, like unto the sad looks of thought-worn widows on a dreary autumnal evening. They are mostly remarkable for the choice of fine words, but lack the freedom of the Japanese language, as they were written in stubborn Chinese characters, with which the authors were not at all familiar.

### Japanese and Chinese Compositions.

Our ancestors could express their ideas and sentiments in language as freely as we moderns can, but as they had only Chinese ideographs in which to write them, their literary compositions were not free or vigorous, as it was very difficult to represent sounds by Chinese characters, which are chiefly symbols for ideas.

For many years after the introduction of Chinese, none but naturalized Chinese or Coreans, or their descendants, were secretaries and clerks in the different offices of the goverment, as it was then customary to prepare all public papers in Chinese. The intercourse between China and Japan became closer and closer as time advanced, and the consequent introduction of Chinese customs, manners, institutions, arts and Buddhism made it necessary for the Japanese to learn to read Chinese books. In time a good knowledge of Chinese literature and philosophy was an indispensable qualification for a Japanese gentleman. The result was, that

Japan produced many scholars who could write Chinese prose or even poetry, as well as if Chinese were their mother tongue. We may indeed say, that to Japan of a thousand years ago Chinese was what Latin was to many countries of Europe in old times.

Even when all writings were prepared in Chinese, the proper nouns could only be represented by the sound of certain ideographs. This borrowing of the sound was gradually extended to other parts of speech till poems and even prose compositions began to appear in the Japanese language in Chinese dress. The Chinese characters thus used were the origin of the *Kana*, of which we have two varieties, respectively called the *Kata Kana* and the *hira-Kana*. At first these *Kana* were unlimited in number, but in time forty-seven of them were selected and arranged in their present order. The *Kana* or *iroha*, so-called after the three initial letters, though born of ideographs, are phonetic letters and much like the European alphabets.

As we have already seen, Chinese was at first the only written language for all purposes, and continued to be used for all important State papers for many years after its general disuse. The use of *Kana* letters, at first limited to *uta*, was in time extended to prose compositions, giving rise to the *Kana-bumi* (*Kana* composition) or *wabun* (Japanese composition), of which many an old master-piece remains. Soon after the full growth of the *Kana-bumi*, it came into vogue to mix Chinese characters among the *Kana*. This led to the formation of the *Kanamajiri-bun*, or Sinico-Japanese language, which is our present written language for all ordinary purposes, public as well as private. Pure Chinese is seldom written except by its professors and students.

### Influence of Scholarly Women in the Development of the Japanese Language.

During the period of unmixed Chinese, no scholarly women were known, excepting the members of the Imperial family, a few ladies of high rank, and nuns. Among the former, the Empresses Koken and Komyo, and a nun named Chiujo-hime, a princess, who became a devout Buddhist, were the most distinguished. Then there was a *Daigaku* (university) at Nara, and a *Kokugaku* (provincial school) in each province. The students, who attended them were sons of government officials, to be themselves employed by the government after graduation. Reading was the chief branch of study at these educational institutions, as it was one of the principal qualifications required of a government official. The weaker sex was permitted no access to these halls of learning.

The other educational institutions of that age, were monasteries and nunneries, where young priests and nuns were instructed in Buddhist literature. There was no public place of education for ordinary women. The scholarship of the pious Empress Komyo was attained through her study of Chinese literature, not for its own sake, but to make herself able to read the Buddhist books.

On the contrary *uta* was composed even in very remote ages by both sexes, and many poems from the pen of ladies are seen in the *Manyo-Collection* containing only those which were composed prior to the time of the Nara government.

For some time after the Nara period the study of Chinese literature was yet in fashion, and history tells us that the Empress Kachi, consort of the Emperor Saga (who reigned 810 to 823 A. D.), and their majesties' daughter, the Princess Uchi, distinguished themselves as Chinese scholars. But the generality of female scholars were composers of *uta*, in which they were not a whit inferior to their literary brothers. The two most distinguished poetesses of the age, under question, were:

### I. ONONOKOMACHI.

The events of her life were not well known. It is, however, certain that she lived in the reign of the Emperor Jimmei (834 to 850 A. D.) and was a very beautiful woman. Many of her poems are given in a book called "*Kokin Waka-shiu*," a collection of ancient and modern poems. They are also published in a separate volume.

### II. ISE NO MIYASUDOKORO.

She lived a little later than Ononokomachi. She was a daughter of Fujiwara Tsugukage, and bore a prince to the Emperor Uda (who reigned 888 to 897 A. D.) as his mistress.

A celebrity both in general literature and Japanese poetry. A collection of her poems is a well-known book.

It is from this period that the Sinico-Japanese language dates. It was at first written only by women, and those men who could not write pure Chinese. The first famous book written in it and now remaining is the *Tosanikki* of Ki no Tsurayuki, who compiled the *Kokin Waka-shiu* in 905, by order of the Emperor Daigo. In the preface to the *Tosanikki*, its author says: "I, a woman, venture to write what has heretofore been attempted by men only." It was made to appear the production of a woman, for no other reason, within our knowledge, than that it was written in the Sinico-Japanese language. In it we find that the men wrote in the Chinese characters and the women in the *Kana*.

Soon after the appearance of the worthy Tosanikki, the Sinico-Japanese became the language of epistolary communications and of light literature. Even men of learning began to use it in letter writing.

The *Monogatari* or 'Tales,' so famous and important in Japanese literature, were all written in this mixed language. The *Taketori Monogatari* or a "Bamboo-cutter's Tale," considered the oldest of its kind, seems to have been written some time before or after the Emperor Daigo's time. The *Utsubo, Yamato* and *Ochikubo Monogatari*, doubtless the productions of the tenth century, though their authoresses are unknown, still remain and are read by all students of Japanese literature. Many other works of the same nature appeared in the reign of the Emperor Daigo, of which nothing but the name now remains.

In the reign of the Emperor Ichijo (987-1011) the use of the Sinico-Japanese was much cultivated by women, and a great many *Monogatari*, diaries, and light literature were published, of which not a few have lived to this day, and are considered as master-pieces, and as models for imitation. By far the most distingnished of these works is the *Genji Monogatari* by Murasaki Shikibu.

### MURASAKI SHIKIBU.

Murasaki Shikibu, the daughter of Fujiwara Tanetoki and wife of Fujiwara Nobutaka, was a born genius. She was unparalleled in all descriptions of feminine virtues. For a considerable length of time after her husband's death she confined herself in a small apartment, wholly dedicating her thoughts to his memory. Afterward she became an inmate of the Imperial Court as a maid of honor to the Empress Consort of the reigning Emperor. Her Majesty's father, Fujiwara Michinaga, took pains to have none but virtuous and learned women in the Imperial chambers. Still Shikibu was a star amongst them. She did or said nothing calculated to show her in any way superior to an ordinary woman. She once explained the *Hakushi Bunshiu* (Hakurakuten's Prose Works), a difficult Chinese book, in the presence of the Empress Ichijo, by her Majesty's special order, a fact that puts it beyond all doubt that she was a learned lady. She was well read not only in Japanese and ordinary Chinese literatures, but also in Buddhist *sutras*, as we may see in several chapters of her undying work, the *Genji Monogatari*. From her childhood she displayed uncommon talents and a decided inclination for learning. While yet very young she sat in her elder brother Korenori's study, listening to his studious reading and committing all he read aloud to memory. This is said to have often called forth the pleasant regret of her father: "Oh! that she were a man!" There are reasons to suppose that she was an excellent musician. It is related in her own *nikki* or diary that she spent many days after her consort's death in reading his writings and playing on her favorite musical instrument.

The Emperor Ichijo one day read her immortal work and observed to his chamberlains that the authoress must have perused the *Nihonki*, or "Japanese Chronicles," a circumstance that earned for her the learned surname of the " *Maid of the Nihonki.*" In her time there were many worthy literary ladies, but she and Seishonagon, were the cynosures among them all. She had two daughters, who served the Emperors Go-Ichijo and Go-Reizen as nurses, proving themselves quite worthy of their mother. The best known of Shikibu's works are the *Genji Monogatari*, the *Murasaki Shikibu Nikki*, and the *Murasaki Shikibu Kashiu*, all of which are even now widely read. The second of these works, originally quite a large volume but now reduced to a mere pamphlet by the theft of time, is a narration of her court life in the form of *nikki* or a diary. Its language is not half so elegant as that of the *Monogatari*, but we meet with many passages in it that show the strength and vigor of the pen of the great authoress.

### Famous Works and Their Authoresses.

A great many old *monagatari*, *nikki*, *uta*, etc., are handed down to us. A few of them may be mentioned:

#### I. THE "KAGERO NO NIKKI."

This is a diary written by the wife of Fujiwara Kanemune, who was premier in the first part of the Emperor Ichijo's reign. It is mainly a history of her conjugal and parental affections. The authoress does not give her real name, but calls herself *the Mother of Michitsuna*, so much does the book relate of her son.

#### II. THE "IDZUMI SHIKIBU NIKKI."

Idzumi Shikibu, a contemporary of Michitsuna's mother, was the daughter of Oye Masamune. She first married Tachibana Michisada, the Lord of Idzumi, who died shortly after marriage. She then entered the Imperial palace to serve the Empress Akiko. She was afterward married to Fujiwara Yasumasa, the Lord of Tango. She stood in the foremost rank among the authoresses and poetesses of her time. Her best known work, the *Idzumi Shikibu Nikki*, relates how the Prince Atsumichi, the son of the Emperor Reizen, sought her love.

#### III. THE "SAGOROMO NIKKI."

This is a production of Daini Sammi Kata-ko, one of the two daughters of the justly famous Murasaki Shikibu. It is much like the immortal work of her mother in diction and in general design.

#### IV. THE "SARASHINA NIKKI."

A diary by the daughter of Uchiuben Sagawara Taka. The authoress married Tachibana Toshimichi. She was an excellent poetess and prose writer. Before her marriage she served the Empress Suke Ko, the daughter of the Emperor Go-Shujaku, who reigned 1027 to 1045.

A diary by Sanuki, the mistress of the Emperor Horikawa (1087 to 1107). It details the agonies and death of her Imperial master, and the Emperor Toba's succession to the throne.

Collections of poems written by the more famous of the old poetesses will be mentioned below:

## VI. THE "MURASAKI SHIKIBU KASHIU; OR, A COLLECTION OF MURASAKI SHIKIBU'S POEMS."

## VII. THE "SEISHONAGON KASHIU AND MAKURA NO SOSHI."

Seishonagon, the daughter of Higo no Kami Kiyowara no Motosuke, served the Empress Sadako, the Consort of the Emperor Ichijo, and distinguished herself among her colleagues by the sprightliness of her disposition, the brilliancy of her talents, and the profundity of her learning. The Empress Sadako was the daughter of Chiu Kwampaku Michitaka, and had been married before her Imperial husband ascended the Throne. It is related in her *Makura no Soshi* that the Empress was an excellent poetess and scholar. Seishonagon was highly beloved of Her Majesty. It is said that the Empress often wished to see this poetess raised to the highest rank of Court service. But before this was carried into effect the Empress' influence in the Court had declined, and what was more, she died, surviving her faded glory only a short space of time. This sad event frustrated all hopes of promotion for the unfortunate favorite. Many a record says that, soon after her patron's death, Seishonagon retired into a house where her deceased father had lived, and there lived in great obscurity, dying at a great age. Others say that it was as a nun in a holy establishment named the Seigwanji that she passed her subsequent life, praying for the repose of her Imperial mistress' soul. Which is the truth it is more than we can ascertain.

Akiko, the new Empress of Ichijo, was no less fond of learned maids of honor than her predecessor, and therefore Seishonagon's erudition, which all her contemporaries frankly declared far above their own, might have found it an easy passport to the Court, if she had so wished. But her high spirit would not be satisfied with less than the greatest favors of her mistress, which she, the recipient of those of the former Empress, could not hope to secure. A passage in the *Makura no Soshi* says: "If it is possible to secure the first rank, be willing to serve; if not, be content with the second or third place."

Her master-piece, the *Makura no Soshi*, was doubtless commenced by her while yet at Court. An old record tells us that she afterward continued and completed it in the pleasurable recollection of her mistress' unparalleled grandeur and her own better days.

### VIII. THE "IDZUMI SHIKIBU KASHIU."
### IX. THE "AKAZOME EMON KASHIU."

Emon was the daughter of Oye Masahira and wife of Akazome Tokimochi. She displayed rare talents and a sincere love of knowledge while yet in infantile years. Her husband, born of a learned family of long standing, was himself an object of universal praise as a gifted scholar. Some time after their union Emon found her husband unusually thoughtful upon his return home from official duty. Inquiring the cause, he thus replied: "His Grace Shijo Kuito, wishes to resign, for what cause I know not, and has had his letter of resignation composed by Ki no Tokina and Oye Mochikoto. The letters they prepared were not quite to his satisfaction, and he has asked me to-day to prepare another for him. If they, who are both scholars of established reputation could not satisfy him, how can I? You see the cause of my thoughtfulness." Upon this, Emon thought a little while and said: "Those gentlemen were vain-glorious. They dwelt on the greatness of their families and the comparative obscurity of their present position. Your writing will be received with an eulogium." It occurred just as she had said. How keen was her insight into men and things! This couple had a son and a daughter who were distinguished for great learning and brilliant talents.

### X. THE "UMA NAIJI SHIU."

The authoress of this collection of *uta* was the daughter of Samano Kami Tokiaki. She was a favorite of the Emperor Ichijo, a contemporary of Akazome Emon and Idzumi Shikibu, and she was quite their equals in poetry.

## XI. THE "TSUNENOBU HAHA SHIU."

The mother of Dainagon Tsunenobu, the authoress of this collection, was the wife of Junii Gon-Chiunagon Minamoto no Michikata. She loved knowledge very much. In training her son, Tsunenobu, she thought that much of his future might depend on the environs of his residence, and accordingly had a house erected close to the Nishi no Doin, where a number of learned professors then lived. Tsunenobu was quite a musician even while a mere boy, doubtless owing to the instructions of his mother, whose musical skill was almost divine. It is related in this book as well as elsewhere that when she once accompanied her father to the Province of Mimasaka, she found a crowd of people assembled in a temple playing a sort of mystery called *singaku* in order to so please the goddess that she would call down the rain from the sky, and that she, a girl of only 12 or 13, immediately thrust herself among the multitude and played on a *biwa* or lute, when the heavens suddenly darkened and down poured a shower, gratifying the people and refreshing the fields.

## XII. THE "DEWA NO BEN SHIU."

The authoress, the daughter of Fujiwara Hidenobu, the Lord of Dewa, was a Court lady in the reign of the Emperor Ichijo.

## XIII. THE "ISE NO OSUKE SHIU."

This poetess, the daughter of Sukechika, the head priest of the Ise Temple, was a contemporary and colleague of Dewa no Ben.

## XIV. THE "KO-OKIMI SHIU."

Another maid of honor at the Emperor Ichijo's Court. She was the daughter of the Prince Shigeaki.

## XV. THE "SAGAMI SHIU."

The daughter of Minamoto no Yorimitsu, and wife of Kinsuke, the Lord of Sagami. The Emperor Juntoku once said that the poetesses Akazome Emon, Murasaki Shikibu and Sagami, were fully worthy to be classed with the ancient bards. This shows what a skillful poetess she was.

### XVI. THE "KAMO NO YASUNORI JO SHIU."

This is the collection of the poems by the second daughter (*Jo*), of Kamo no Yasunori, the famous astronomer. The authoress enjoyed an enviable reputation for the brilliancy of her talents.

### XVII. THE "BEN NO NIUBO SHIU."

The authoress, a daughter of Murasaki Shikibu, was nurse (*niubo*) to the Emperor Reizen (who reigned 1046 to 1068) when his majesty was an infant.

### XVIII. THE "YUSHI NAISHINNO KE KII SHIU."

Daughter of Sammi Taira no Tsunekata, and the younger sister of Shigetsune, the Lord of Kii. She called herself Kii, after the name of her brother's estate, and Yushi Naishinno Ke, for she served in the household (*Ke*), of the Princess (*naishinno*) Yushi, the daughter of the Emperor Shujaku, the son of the Emperor Go-Reizen.

### XIX. THE "KO-JIJIU SHIU."

Daughter of Mitsukiyo, a pensioner of the Iwashimidzu. Her mother, named Ko-Daishin, was an excellent poetess. Ko-Jijiu served the retired Emperor and Empress in the reign of the Emperor Takakura (1169 to 1180). She was surnamed Matsuyoi no Jijiu, because of her having composed a happy poem on a *matsu-Yoi*, or the fourteenth of a lunar month (literally, *waiting evening*).

### XX. THE "YASUSUKE NO HAHA SHIU."

The authoress was the wife of Minamoto no Nobuyoshi, the grandson of the Emperor Kwazan, and mother of the Prince Yasusuke. Her son was adopted by the Prince Kiyohito, another of his grandfathers. He afterward succeeded to his father's office, the Directorship of Divine Rites, which situation was bestowed on him as inheritable.

### XXI. THE "NIJO DAIWO DAIKOGU DAINI SHIU."

The daughter of Dazai Daini Takashina Shigeaki, this authoress served the Princess Reishi, the lady honored as mother of the Emperor Toba (who reigned 1108 to 1123). Her mistress lived in the Nijo palace, and after the birth of her daughter was crowned and venerated as Daiwo Daikogu (Her Majesty the Empress Dowager); hence the name of the authoress.

### XXII. THE "JIKENMONIN HORIKAWA SHIU."

This poetess was the daughter of Akinaka, the Director of Divine Rites. She served Jikenmonin, the Consort of the Empress Toba. Her fame as a poetess was great. It is mentioned in this collection that she survived her husband, but who he was is unknown.

### XXIII. THE "NIJOIN SANUKI SHIU."

Sanuki was the daughter of Sammi Minamoto no Yorimasa and served the Emperor Nijo (who reigned 1159 to 1165). It is the opinion of Teikakyo that she was not inferior to Iyetaka in poetic skill. She was often reputed as versed in Chinese classics.

### XXIV. THE "KENREIMONIN UKYODAYU SHIU."

The authoress, Ukyodayu, was the daughter of Tomomasa and served the Empress Kenreimonin, the Consort of the Emperor Takakura. She was a celebrated poetess and musician. She afterward became a nun and called herself Yugiri no Ama.

### XXV. THE "TOSHINARIKYO JO SHIU:"

The authoress was the daughter of Toshinarikyo, a master poet. She had brilliant parts and was a great poetess. Her beauty was the topic of the day. One day she was informed that the plum trees in the garden of a neighboring temple were in full bloom. She went alone to enjoy the lovely blossoms, in dirty disguise. Questionable young men came close to her, much to her annoyance. She therefore turned her paces homeward, when the scapegraces, little dreaming who she was, began calling her names, and pointing to her shabby garments, quite a contrast to her beautiful features. She then extemporarized a poem which revealed her real self, upon which the rogues took to their heels in utter confusion. Not a few of her poems were taken into several Imperial compilations. In old age she became a nun and secluded herself in her estate at Koshibe; hence her popular surname of " Koshibe no Zenni" or the *nun of Koshibe of the Zen belief.*

## Literature After the Middle Ages.

In the middle ages of our history, the members of the Fujiwara family had the reins of government in their hands. Seeing their power firmly established, they resorted to every form of luxurious extravagance, and were entirely absorbed in sensuality and sloth. The Court and the town were only too glad to follow the manners of their real rulers. Drinking parties and concerts were enjoyed by almost every man and woman. Fine language was cultivated by all classes, high and low. Great pride was felt in competing with each other in wit and humor. No person made use of words or phrases until well considered. Many worthy poetesses and authoresses appeared at this time.

But when the provincial warriors came into power about 1150, the influence of the courtiers declined and literature, which they so greatly patronized, lost much of its splendor. Half a century later we find the muses cultivated only by the tender sex. It happened not infrequently that the Court ladies teased their gentleman colleagues by asking them learned questions, which required some erudition to answer. In this age when men were generally illiterate, many worthy books were written by women, of which some remain:

### THE BEN NAIJI NIKKI.

A collection of poems in the form of a diary. It extends from the coronation of the Emperor Go-Fukakusa in 1246 to 1252. The authoress was the daughter of Fujiwara Nobuzane and a maid of honor to the Emperor Go-Fukakusa.

### THE NAKATSUKASA NAIJI NIKKI.

The authoress, the daughter of Fujiwara Nagatsune, entered into Court service a little later than Ben Naiji. This diary extends from 1280 to 1292. Nakatsukasa Naiji wrote a great many poems, which are collected in a volume.

Famous as these books are, the best known of all the literary productions by women of the thirteenth century and the various works by Abutsuni.

Abutsuni had splendid talents and shone in various departments of literature, especially in Japanese poetry. Her father was a feudal lord, Sado no Kami Taira no Norishige by name. When young she served Ankamonin, the Consort of the Emperor Juntoku, and then called herself Shijo or Uemon no Suke. Abutsuni was her name after she took the Buddhist vows.

Her husband, Fujiwara Tameiye, was the son of Sandaiye, and grandson of Toshinari, both of whom were what answer to the poets laureate of the English Crown. He himself suceeded to the literary office of his ancestors, and compiled the Zoku Gosenshiu and the Zoku Kokinshiu. He bestowed on his infant son an estate named Hosokawa, in the Province of Harima, when on his death-bed. But since Tamesuke, for that was the infant's name, could not possibly manage the estate, Tameuji, his brother on the paternal side, was intrusted with its government. As too often happens in like cases, Tameuji would not return the estate, whereupon Abutsuni went down to Kamakura in person and submitted the case to Hojo Tokimune for decision. Tokimune then held the full powers of the State, except a mere show of subserviency to the Emperor. Abutsuni thus saw the estate returned to its rightful owner, and tradition says she there passed her last days. This traveling from Kamakura to Kyoto gave her a topic for a beautiful diary styled the *Jiuroku Ya Nikki* (literally rendered *sixteen nights' diary*), which appeared in 1280.

Tamesuke became a good poet, reflecting great credit upon his ancestors, who had often held the office of poets laureate. He was also installed in his father's hereditary office. His family name was Reizen.

Abutsuni had a daughter named Ki no Naiji, who was justly famous as a poetess.

Was it not remarkable that she made bold to present herself before the august personage, who was a sovereign all but nominally, and that for nothing greater than the settlement of a family feud? Let this query be answered by another. How could our poetry have been kept so elevated and beautiful so many hundreds of stormy years if she had not placed the Reizen family above want by restoring to the family the Hosokawa estate and so enabling them to lead the literary world for so long a period?

Abutsuni wrote the *Niwa no Nishiki* and the *Yakwaku Shiu* for her daughter's moral and literary education. These works prove her to have been an excellent mother.

The *Niwa no Nishiki* details what a true woman is. It is a model which every person would do well to study. The *Yakwaku Shiu* is a critical treatise on the poems of the various Imperial collections. It shows her to have been an able dialectician. Two other products of her pen are praiseworthy. One is the *Utatane*, a sort of autobiography, which possesses high literary merit. The other is a series of prayers she wrote for the salvation of her deceased husband. The pathos running through the whole volume is so great as to draw a shower of tears from all who read it.

When, early in the seventeenth century, Tokugawa Iyeyasu conquered the whole country, and found himself its ruler all but in name, he used all his endeavors to awake the nation to the importance of learning. This commendable work of the great Shogun caused a crowd of poets and scholars to appear. The learning of this *renaissance* period differed from that of the Fujiwara age, mainly in the two following points :

First. In the latter period learning was literature, and literature was learning, but in the former, the term learning signified more, being used for many new sciences, among the rest politics, ethics, philosophy and economics.

Second. Formerly it was only persons of quality who studied, and for their personal amusement. In the Tokugawa period even those in the lower grades of society began to learn but less for the sake of amusement and more for the sake of utility.

At the Revival of Letters the Confucian doctrine of 'women under men' gained such an ascendency as to make the comparative ignorance of the women anything but uncommon, save in the poetic art. As was only natural, however, to this highly literary age there then lived a number of distinguished female scholars, among whom Kaibara Hatsu-Ko and Otakasaka Isa-Ko are worthy of especial notice.

Kaibara Hatsu-Ko, the wife of Kaibara Ekkeu (1630-1714), was one of the most celebrated Chinese scholars Japan ever produced, and was also highly accomplished and virtuous. She traveled far and wide together with her husband, who served the Lord of Chikuzen, and made himself justly famous by his works on popular education, most of which it was wise of him to write in the easiest possible style. It is a well ascertained fact that Hatsu-Ko assisted her husband not a little in his literary pursuits.

Otakasaka Isa-Ko, wife of Otakasaka Shizan (1649-1713), was a Japanese and Chinese scholar. Her husband was one of the most learned men of his time and was a vassal of the Lord of Inaba. Isa-Ko wrote the *Kara Nishiki*, a great work of thirteen volumes, in compliance with an especial request of her husband's suzerain. The *Kara Nishiki* is a full treatise on female education and etiquette. Comprehensive and beautiful as it is, she prepared it within so short a space of time as three months. We ask for no other information before we judge her a rare mistress of letters.

Besides these two, Arakida Reiko, a noted historian and poetess, Ando Kame Ko, surnamed the Modern Shikibu, Rozenni, of whom we have spoken at some length under "Religion," Takashima Bunho, Inouye Micho, and a few others made their names more or less known by their Chinese as well as Japanese learning in the earlier years of the Tokugawa Shogunate.

In the Bunsei period, which began with the year 1818, then lived one Takashima Yahei at Kojimachi, in Tokyo, of whose daughter we are now going to speak. When very young she already displayed rare talents, and a decided love of books. Her father allowed her young mind to follow its natural bent, and in time she made herself a great mistress of literature and the various feminine accomplishments, such as tea-making, *hanaike* (the art of arranging flowers in vases), etc. Hundreds of the maids of honor serving in the Tokugawa household sent to receive instructions from her in poetry and other refined arts, a distinction that could not fail to make her famous.

When quite young Bunho was prevailed upon by her father to marry a certain man. She became as dutiful a wife as a woman could, until an accident occurred which caused her to separate from her husband and live single the remainder of her life. One day a reunion was held on the second floor of her residence. After the guests went away, she was carrying the plates down stairs when she lost her footing on a high step of the staircase and fell headlong upon the ground floor. Her husband, who was yet upstairs, looked at her and asked, not if she were hurt, but if any china was broken. This she thought unnatural and unkind, and forthwith had her parents agree to the severance of the conjugal connections.

Her manners were extremely gentle and elegant, and her mind was correspondingly strong and manly. One day she was out walking in Muko Yanagiwara, when a pickpocket followed her closely and furtively. She caught sight of the rogue but showed no signs of discovery or alarm. With a presence of mind rarely seen in one of her sex, Bunho unfastened a silver hairpin as secretly as possible and was throwing it at the thief's eye, when the astonished villain took to flight in all haste.

### ENOUYE MICHI-KO.

Enouye Michi-Ko, the daughter of Enouye Manemon, a Sanuki *samurai*, and wife of Mita Moemon, displayed high literary talents long before she was of age and composed Japanese and Chinese poems very skillfully. When 18 she traveled to Edo in the suite of the lady of her father's liege lord, and wrote the *Tokai Kiko;* or, "East Sea Travels." Nine years later she returned home to Sanuki and then wrote another book of travels called the *Kika Nikki;* or, "Homeward Diary." She afterward married Mita Moemon, one of her father's friends. Her son, Yoshikatsu by name, became a famous scholar, quite worthy of his learned mother. Michi-Ko lived to see him honored with a tutorship to the Lord of

Sanuki. Her poems collected in a volume named the *Oji Shiu* and her *Travels*, still remain.

## CONCLUSION.

Our present literary galaxy has some very bright stars, but these we leave to later writers to describe.

The foregoing pages are intended to tell what women have done towards the advancement of literature in our country.

Were it not extremely difficult to translate Japanese into English we would have given some of the gems of the different authoresses of whom we have spoken. In our opinion, anything like a readable translation of literary master-pieces from one into the other of so widely different languages as the two in question, is simply next to impossible.

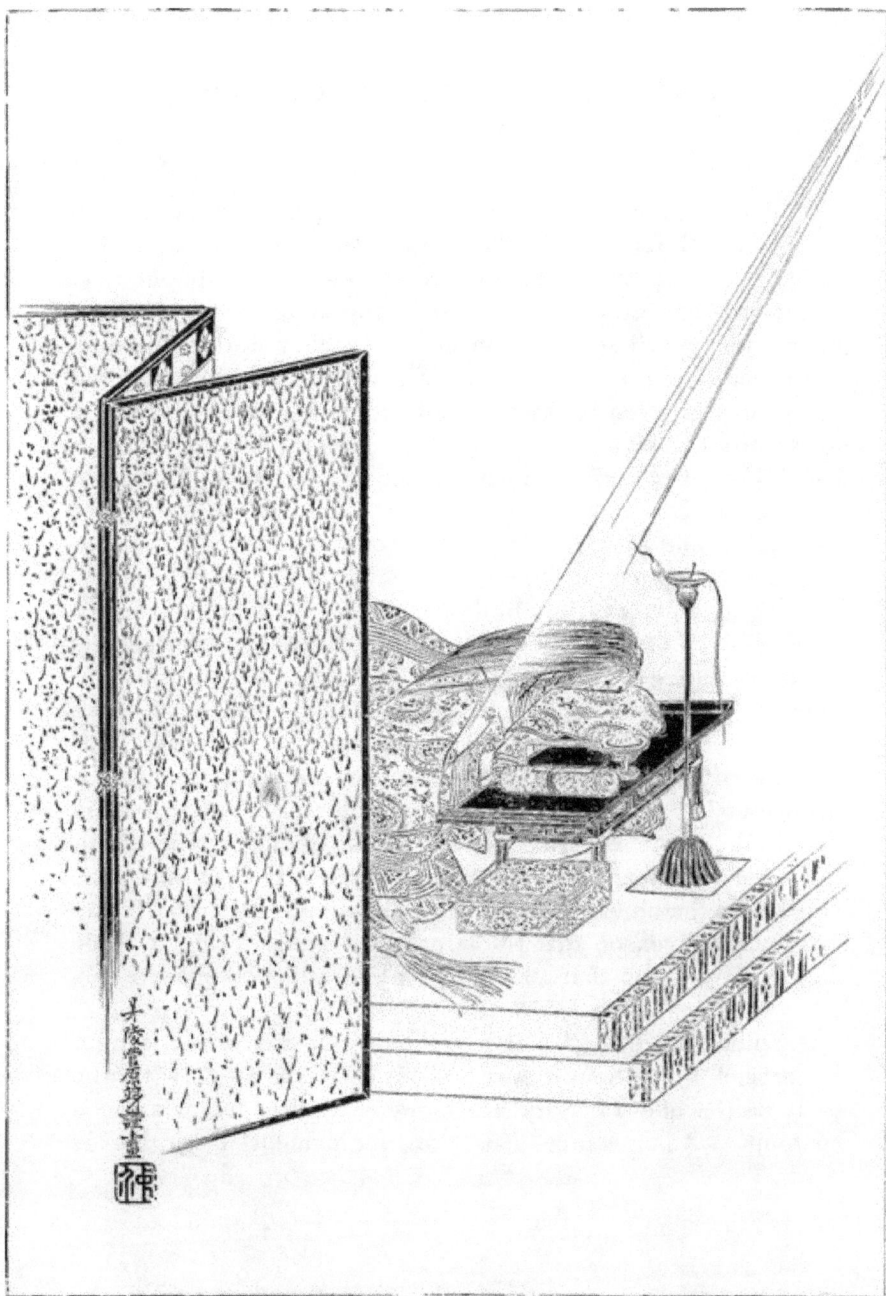

# CHAPTER IV.

## JAPANESE WOMEN IN RELIGION.

The religions, and what pass as religions, now existing in Japan are Shintoism, Confucianism, Buddhism, and Christianity. Among them Buddhism stands first in popularity. Shintoism has numerous believers and temples, but it is a misnomer to call it a religion, for it teaches nothing of man after death nor of aught that is profound. It has not had power enough even to assert its independence since the middle ages, often allowing the Buddhist priests to encroach on its rights. Coufucianism, too, is not a religion, as it teaches nothing but morality and politics based upon the sayings' of Confucius and his disciples. The remaining two, it is needless to say, are true religions.

Christianity has its abiding place in the hearts of only a small portion of the nation, despite the strenuous efforts of its modern evangelists, mainly because it offended the Government and the people, when it was first introduced, some three hundred years ago, not because of its doctrines or rites, but because of the inordinate ambition of its propagators. Buddhism was introduced into Japan more than a thousand years ago, and is believed in by a great majority of the people, and has been the means of greatly enlightening their minds, and it remains the chief religion even at present. It is not, therefore, without reason that the lalns and virtues of wonien to be dealt with in this chapter are chiefly in connection with this religion.

Shintoism, though not a religion, as said above, cannot be passed by without a word, as it concerns itself with the early deities of our history, and many of its rites follow antique customs. An instance was the employment of virgins as priestesses. This custom is no longer in vogue, but, in ancient times the greater part of the temples had Imperial Princesses as superintendents of rites. When an Imperial Princess was to be sent to the Great Temple of Ise, a temporary office, with a staff of more than a hundred officials, was established in the Imperial Court for the performance of a series of ceremonies to free her from human uncleanness. Once created the *Saishu* (superintendent of rites) she was considered as sacred and was highly respected. The Kamo Temple at Kyoto had at one time the same sacred superintendents, and the Imperial office established for the management of affairs concerning these superintendents was called the Kamo Ceremonies Bureau. This employment of virgins as superintendents was also in vogue amongst the common people. The *Omonoimisama* of the Kashima Temple in the Province of Hitachi was an instance. From among the people living under the protection of the god worshiped in this temple, or *ujiko*, a girl under 7 years of age was selected, and after duly asking the god whether she would satisfy the divine will, she was made to reside in a beautiful house built beside the temple. Her dresses, food and other necessaries were offered her as respectfully and reverentially as if she were herself a goddess. But when she attained maturity, she was displaced by another young girl. Thus the term of this holy service varied from a few months to several years. After returning to their homes, they lived and married like ordinary women.

Besides the high service above stated, these young girls served the various gods and goddesses as dancers, musicians, and necromancers. They were called *miko* or *uneme*. In marriage and other human affairs, they in nowise differed from their lay sisters.

### BUDDHISM.

The Buddhist religion is not yet known to the Europeans and Americans in its true light. Their scholars too often write of it not unlike one who speaks of the interior of a mansion while standing at its gate. This is not, however, so much due to the want of their investigations, as to the diversity of the ways in which it has been explained. Shakamuni, himself, taught it in five different ways in his life, and his disciples taught one or another of these five in three more different ways, thus giving rise to a great number of sects and schools. Of these what has been introduced to Europe is the doctrine of a sect of the *Hinayana* or Smaller Development, while it is one of the *Mahayana* or Greater Development that has had the greatest number of devotees in Japan.

The *Shingon*, otherwise named the *Yoga* or *Guhya*, the most profound of Buddhist teachings, is a highly comprehensive doctrine. It looks upon all religious and ethical principles with an equal eye, is inpenetrable to mere book readers, and is unfathomable to all except those who have listened as its great teachers have explained its nicer principles. Manifold as are the ways in which Buddhism is taught, each and all of them lead one to a profound understanding of Buddha. The length of time required for study and meditation must vary according to the ability of each devotee.

The principal sects in Japan are:

I. Two of the *Hinayana:*
    (1)  The *Kusha* or *Ushu.*
    (2)  The *Jojitsu* or *Kushu.*

II. Five of the *Mahayana:*
    (1)  The *Hoso.*
    (2)  The *Sauron.*
    (3)  The *Tentai.*
    (4)  The *Kegon.*
    (5)  The *Shingon.*

Of the five *Mahayana* sects, the *Hoso* and *Sanron* are classed as the *Gon Daijo* or *Preliminary Mahayana*, they being introductory to the *Jitsu Daijo* or *Real Mahayana;* the *Tentai* and *Kegon* as the *Jitsu Daijo*, and the *Shingon* as the *Himitsu Daijo* or *Secret Mahayana.*

The *Tentai* has five subdivisions, viz.: The *Yuzu-nembutsu-shiu, Jodo-shiu, Shin-shiu, Nichiren-shiu*, and *Ji-shiu.*

There is another sect called *Zen-shiu*, emanating from the *Hoso* and *Tentai*. Still another sect called *Ris-shiu* has some devotees. Though the Buddhists are divided into these and several other sects, yet all of them agree in the fundamental principle, which is to study the law of cause and effect in the moral sphere of human life. They differ among one another:

1. In the extent of the treatment, some limiting it to material things and others extending it to immaterial things.

2. In the depth and width of the treatment of immaterial things.

NUNS.

The reasons upon which the *Mahayana* and *Hinayana* sects base the admission of women into the priesthood differ in some respects. The latter sect asserts that Shakamuni had not permitted any woman to take the vows before *Gantami*, his aunt, requested him to receive her as a priestess after the death of her husband, which request he declined at first, but to which he was afterward prevailed upon to consent by one of his disciples named Anan, on condition of her keeping the following eight rules:

1. A nun, though as venerably old as a century, shall pay respect at the feet of even a mere neophyte of the opposite sex.

2. A nun shall not censure a priest.

3. A nun shall not find fault with a priest.

4. A nun shall be instructed in the forty-eight Commandments by a priest.

5. A nun shall confess her faults (if any) to a priest.

6. A nun shall listen to a priest's sermon every half month.

7. A nun shall subject herself to a three-months' retirement in the spring or summer months, under the inspection of a priest.

8. A nun shall confess her faults or request others to mention them after the said retirement.

In Japan the priests and nuns who have been fully possessed of the Buddhist Commandments are respectively called *biku* and *bikuni*, after the Sanskrit words, *bikuchu* and *bikuchuni*.

The Commandments for nuns are 277 in some sects and 348 in others.

Among the 348, the following eight are the most important, and are called *harai* after the Sanskrit word *pharajika*, or major crimes:

1. Do not perpetrate any unclean act.

2. Do not steal anything belonging to another.

3. Do not commit murder; do not make another commit murder; do not praise a murderer.

4. Do not call one's self a sage without an amount of knowledge and wisdom worthy of that name.

5. Do not touch any part of a man's body entertaining any amorous sentiment toward him.

6. A nun shall not grasp the hand of a man that she knows to love her, or catch his garment, or go with him behind a screen, or talk with him, or lean upon his body, or appoint a time to meet him.

7. A nun shall not conceal another's faults, when she and her religious sisters take the vows and make public confessions.

8. A nun shall not live in a monastery with monks, before she has taken the monastic vows.

A nun who has broken any one of these eight Commandments is degraded, and is condemned, after her death, to an immense amount of pain in purgatory for 1,100,060,000 years.

II. Seventeen of these rules are called *sozan* or *sogyabashisha* after the Sanskrit *sareghadisesa*. There are certain penances by which retributions may be avoided, but before these penances are achieved, a guilty nun is forbidden to officiate in any holy service.

III. Two hundred and eight in number are called *shadatsu* or *nisatsugihaitsudai* (Sanskrit, *naisarghika*).

IV. Eight in number are called *taisetsu* or *haradaidaishani* after the Sanskrit *pratidisanya*.

V. One hundred in number are called *shiugaku* or *chukira* (Sanskrit, *sikchakarami*).

VI. Seven in number are called *messo*. These are for avoiding disputes.

The punishment due to any but the first twenty-five of these Commandments may be avoided by devotional confessions or penances.

Although these Commandments are for the *Hinayana* nuns, yet they are often kept by the more strictly disciplined ones of the *Hamayana* sects.

In the *Hamayana* doctrine it is the mind that is made the object of teaching and therefore the distinction of sex is not considered in its devotees.

The *Mahayana* priests and nuns generally keep the same Commandments as do the *Hinayana* ones, but it is the ten major and forty-eight minor Commandments mentioned in the *Bon-mo-kyo* (Sanskrit, *Brahmaghala Sutra*) that are observed by the more strict of the *Mahayana* ecclesiastics. The latter, though considerably fewer than those of the *Hinayana* denominations, are much harder to keep. To illustrate this by an example, it constitutes a murder only to desire to kill a man according to the *Mahayana* doctrine, while according to the *Hinayana*, it does not, until one is actually killed.

The ten major Commandments are:

1. Do not kill a living creature with pleasure.
2. Do not steal.
3. Do not gratify the sexual passion.
4. Do not be talkative with an object in view.
5. Do not sell any alcoholic beverage.
6. Do not talk about the faults of others.
7. Do not praise yourself or vituperate others.
8. Do not be covetous of any doctrine or law; do not insult it.
9. Do not indignantly reject an apology.
10. Do not depreciate Buddha, Buddhism, or Monks.

The *Hinayana* schools aim at the salvation or entry into the *Nirvana* of the learners, while the *Mahayana* make it their chief object to get others saved, that is, to induce them to enter *Nirvana*. This essential difference between the two doctrines is to be observed in their disciplinary rules.

There are three divisions of the *Tendai* sect:

1. The *Zen-shiu*.
2. The *Hokke-shiu*.
3. The *Jodo-shiu*.

The last has a sub-sect called *Shin-shiu*.

The *Zen-shiu*, the main doctrine of which is to understand the world as vacant and everything as nothing, was first promulgated in this country at the end of the twelfth century by Eisai Zenshi, who had learned Buddhism in China. The means by which the followers of his school think it possible to understand the truth *in their fashion*, is the *zazen*, or sitting with crossed legs in profound meditation.

The *Hokke-shiu*, founded by Nichiren in the middle of the thirteenth century, has its doctrine based upon the teachings of Buddha contained in the Sutra, called *Hokke-Kyo* or *Sadhor-mapundarika*. This school teaches that the only means for attaining religious enlightenment is the repeated perusal of the holy book just mentioned.

The *Jodo-shiu*, or Pure Land sect, founded by Honen, has for its main doctrine to aim at a second birth in the *Gokuraku*, or *Sukhavati* (Pure Land or Paradise), by the repeated recitation of the name of *Amida Butsu* or *Buddha Amikabha*.

The *Shin-shiu* is the same as the *Jodo-shiu* in every respect, except it does not forbid the priests to eat meat and to have wives.

All these sects, except the *Shin-shiu*, have nuns.

The lower classes of this country are mostly believers in the *Hokke* and *Shin-shiu*, for the means they teach for leading one to Paradise, are the easiest.

### THE NOMENCLATURE OF NUNS.

A woman who has left her home and entered a nunnery is generally called *bikuni* after the Sanskrit word *bikchuni*.

A nun who has not yet taken the full vows is called *shamini* (in Sanskrit, *Scramanerika*); one who has entered a nunnery and is taking lessons in the rites, by which she is to be ordained a *bikuni*, is named *shikishamana*, after the Sanskrit word *Sikchamana*, which name is not known among the laity and only seldom used even in nunneries at present.

Lay women not living in a nunnery but firmly believing in Buddhism, sometimes took the five vows, of not killing any living creature; not stealing; not gratifying the sexual passion unlawfully; not being talkative; and not drinking any alcoholic beverage. These were called *yubai* after the Sanskrit word *upasika*. Such women were not rare in ancient times and some of them went so far as to abstain from marriage, and even to perform some religious services. At present they are very rarely seen and even the name yubai is well nigh forgotten.

Nuns live in nunneries and there educate novices just as monks live in monasteries and educate probationers. Formerly the greater monasteries and nunneries did not forbid members of the opposite sex to live on the same ground, but when the Restoration occurred, it was followed by a general decrease of morality among the monks, and objections arose which resulted in excluding all women from monasteries.

The clothing of nuns is like that of monks. They shave their heads and anything of an ornamental nature is prohibited. They do not blacken their teeth and shave their eyebrows, as is customary among some lay women. They do not use perfumed waters or carry scent-bags.

A nunnery is presided over by a head nun, but the right of appointing or dismissing the presiding nun and all other important rights are held by the head monk of the sect to which the nunnery belongs.

Nuns can visit monasteries for worship, but they can never assist in the religious services there performed. Monks are sometimes invited to a nunnery to perform certain holy rites. Even in this case, no nun is permitted to officiate in any part of the service.

### RELIGIOUS WORTHIES.

The mother of a family generally has more to do with the home culture of children than has the father; it therefore follows that pious mothers have pious children. The prosperity of religion is thus seen to depend much upon women.

We have had a number of ladies of high birth, who have done much to make Buddhism prosper in this land, by building monasteries and giving subsidies to the clergy.

The Empress Suiko was one of them. It was in her reign that Buddhism was first put fairly on the pathway to prosperity in Japan. Prince Shotoku, Regent, was a wise and learned man and a firm believer in Buddhism; and the Premier, Soga Mumako Sukune, was also a devout Buddhist. They must have done much for the benefit of Buddhism, but it would not have attained the prosperity it then enjoyed, had it not been for the strenuous efforts of the Empress.

Among the twelve sovereigns, who reigned a century after Suiko, five were Empresses, all of whom were the protectors of Buddhism, especially the last or Koken Tenno.

The Empress Koken, the daughter of the Emperor Shomu and Empress Komyo, both devout Buddhists, did all the national treasury could afford for the propagation of Buddhism. It is painful, however, to say that her love of religion went so far as to cause her to become a nun, and to give high official positions to the priests, not without producing injurious results. Her mother, so wise and benevolent that she was surnamed the "Nation's Mother," caused what were called provincial monasteries and provincial nunneries to be built in every province. She built a number of towers in Nara, then the capital of the Empire, and, indeed, it was in her time that the celebrated Daibutsu of the Todaiji was raised. She stands glorious in history as the originator of two benevolent institutions, the poorhouse and the dispensary. It is to be regretted that the regulations of these establishments have not come down to us.

. As one travels through the different provinces of Japan one may see ruined towers, old corner stones, ancient tiles, etc., etc., in or near each of the ancient capital cities of the provinces. These are mostly the remains of the provincial monasteries and nunneries raised by the order of this benevolent and religious Empress.

Before building a provincial monastery she ordered each province to make a gold image of Shakamuni Butsu, sixteen feet in height, and to prepare the 600 volumes of the *Dai-hannya-kyo* or *Malia Prajna Paramita* to be afterward placed in the monastery. Each monastery had a seven-storied tower or *stupo* attached to it. In the tower there were to be placed ten transcribed copies of both the *Kinkwomyo-sai-showo-kyo* or *Suvarna prabhasottama raja Sutra* and *Myoho-renge-kyo* or *Sadharma pundarika sutra*, besides a copy of the former in gilt letters.

How grand these monasteries must have been may be inferred from an Imperial rescript of the following import:

"The monastery is to be the ornament of the province. A good site is a necessary desideratum. If near to houses, no bad odors should come into it. If far, it should not be made onerous for the people to visit it. The Governor should see that the rules of art and health are well observed."

Each monastery had fifty families taxed at its pleasure, and 100 *cho* (about 250 acres) of rice fields bestowed upon it and each nunnery fifty *cho* of rice fields. The former was to have twenty monks and the latter ten nuns.

These monasteries and nunneries varied in size and grandeur in different provinces, but those nearest to Nara were in general the largest and grandest. The To-daiji, then called *So-kokubuji* or Presiding Provincial Monastery, was to control all the other provincial monasteries.

The Empress was skillful in composition and chirography, especially in the latter art, in which she is considered one of the three greatest mistresses Japan has ever produced. She invited celebrated hand writers of her time to her court and made them prepare the *Issai-kyo* on scented paper, the result of which was the production of the famous book known to all lovers of old things as the Empress Komyo's Sutra. A traveler in Yamato will see a number of old religious structures, which will recall this pious Empress to his mind. In the propagation of Buddhism in Japan she stands, not only among women, but also among men, next to the greater patriarchs.

We shall next give a short notice of the Empress Danrin, the Consort of the Emperor Saga, who ascended the Throne some forty years after the death of the Empress Koken. She was very pious and benevolent. She built the Danrin-ji as a home for educated nuns. She had once a number of exquisitely ornamented *Kesa* or scarfs prepared, and sent a priest, Egaku by name, to China to give them to Chinese priests. She became a nun herself when her son, the Emperor Jinmei, was dangerously sick, to pray for his recovery, so devout was her belief in Buddhism. Such as it was, her daughter, the Consort of the Emperor Junna, was also a pious Buddhist. She shaved her head and became a nun after the demise of her husband. She also celebrated a great mass for securing his salvation and disposed of her jewels and clothing to obtain money to be spent in holy offerings. She then converted an old palace at Saga into a monastery, and near it built a charity hospital for monks and nuns, and made the

Junna palace a residence for the nuns serving her. She sent *Kesa* and other things to a monastery called the Kokusei-ji in China for use in religious rites there performed, in memory of Chisha Daishi, the founder of the Tendai sect. More is said of this Empress under "Politics."

In the Fujiwara period of Japanese history there were many Empresses and court ladies who were as religious as the Empress Danrin and her daughter. Indeed, there lived no Empress or court lady of high rank then but built one or more monasteries or nunneries. In the chivalrous and feudal period following this religions as well as literary enlightenment, no such ladies appeared, until the Tokagawa Shoguns firmly grasped the reins of government and restored the old state of things, when there appeared a great many women, high and low, who made themselves conspicuous in the religious world. Of these Keisho-in Ichii (Ichii means first rank) is the best known.

Keisho-in Ichii, a mistress of Iyemitsu, the third of the Tokugawa line, was a daughter of a poor grocer of Kyoto, Jinzaemon by name. When she was yet young, her father died, leaving another daughter and a son. Thereupon her mother was pressed by poverty and made Tama, as she was called, a servant to Mume San, a daughter of Arizumi, a *Kuge*, who served as a high court lady to the eldest daughter of Nobufusa, who was then the Prime Minister of the Emperor. She accompanied her mistress to Edo, now called Tokyo, when the latter went there with the premier's daughter, who was the wife of the third Shogun. Iyemitsu was struck with Tama's remarkable intelligence and made her his mistress, humble as she was. She gave birth to a son, the third of Iyemitsu's in 1646. When the child Tsunayoshi, as it was called, was at the helpless age of 3, his father died. Tsunayoshi was afterward created a great *daimyo* and the poor grocer's daughter found herself mother of a feudal lord. The two other sons of the Shogun had died one after the other and Tsunayoshi was made the Shogun in 1681, when he raised his mother to the first rank of the peerage. Though born of humble parents, she was well read in Confucius' and Buddah's books, and her son was consequently quite a scholar. She was a devout Buddhist. One day she called the Shogun's financial minister to her presence and asked him how much it would take to bury her, if she died. Upon hearing that it would require some hundred thousand dollars, she requested Tsunayoshi to give her that sum before her death, on condition that her burial ceremonies need not be anything more expensive than those of an ordinary woman. Tsunayoshi, who was distinguished for his filial piety, granted her request. She spent the great sum she thus obtained in repairing the oldest religious structures in the province of Yamato. The repairs now shown in several monasteries in Yamato are traceable to the piety and benevolence of this woman.

Besides this she did much for the advancement of Buddhism and learning, as well as for alleviating the pains of the needy.

Women have done much for Buddhism, not only in being its illustrious patrons, but also in supplying it with not a few worthy devotees and nuns, among whom Riozen of the *Zen* sect is the most celebrated. She was truly a woman in form, but a man in mind. The *Zen* nuns' popularity at present owes much to the wise and benevolent conduct of this religious lady.

Riozen was born in Kyoto and when young served as a maid of honor in the To-fuku-mon-in Palace. She was equaled by no woman of her time in beauty. In general learning, in prose and poetic compositions, in the knowledge of Buddhist doctrines, especially of the Zen sect, she was a profound scholar.

When she married a physician, Yasuwara by name, she requested her bridegroom to allow her to retire after she had borne him three or four children. Yasuwara, who was a great Confucian scholar, and quite unmindful of the ordinary affairs of the world, easily granted this request. At the age of thirty she had borne three children and then she left her husband, shaved her head, and put on a *kesa*, that is, became a nun, all but residing in a nunnery.

She afterward went about the country visiting one monastery after another of her favorite sect, asking questions about the difficulties she met with in her devotional studies. In 1681, she saw Hakuo-Osho in Edo (now Tokyo). The great Buddhist gave no reply to her questions, and sent her away from the monastery where he stayed, saying that her beauty was too great for a pure religious life and that a woman should not be seen in so holy a place. Thus driven away she went to the house of an acquaintance, burned her face with a red-hot poker, and composed a Chinese and a Japanese poem both containing the following idea:

"Once a maid of honor, I burned incense in the Imperial chambers. Now a forlorn Buddhist, I burn my face with red iron. The changes of the weather are nothing to be compared to those our lives may experience."

She revisited Hakuo-Osho with these poems. The latter was struck with the strength of her spirit, and the firmness of her determination and instructed her in all the secrets of Buddhism. After that her devotion grew stronger and her morality purer. She then built a nunnery at Ochiai near Edo and called it the Taiunji. In this sanctuary she preached and taught and died. Before her time the *Zen* sect had the smallest number of nuns, for its doctrine is the hardest to understand, and its rules the most difficult to observe. But since her day, it has gained, and consists at present of large numbers of women, some highly famous for their profundity of learning and purity of conduct, chiefly owing to her illustrious and admirable example.

Japan had, and has a number of women patrons and workers in the establishment and support of moral and educational institutions, but their names will not be mentioned here, as they do not bear direct relation to religion.

In Shintoism there may have been some women who did much in its propagation, but their names are unknown to the public, perhaps, because their work was comparatively light.

In Christianity it is not to be doubted that there were many brave women who worked hard and died as martyrs. But since this religion was strictly forbidden under the Tokugawa government, they were punished as ordinary criminals and it cannot be too much regretted that their names are lost in oblivion.

### LAY WOMEN IN RELIGION AND RELIGIOUS SISTERHOODS.

There are two reasons why in nine cases out of ten women of ordinary moral intelligence believe in religious sisterhoods.

1. So they may live an easy life and be saved from all worldly anxieties.

2. To more easily gain Paradise after death.

It is not the teaching of Buddhism that one should believe in it, for such objects as these, but, if, by believing in it, one can enhance her standard of morality, it is well to do so for the good of the world, if not for any other reason.

The religious duties performed by the Buddhists are:

*a.* Each Buddhist family has a certain temple, in whose graveyard its deceased members are buried. On the anniversary of a death that has occurred in the family some member or members of it visit the temple and have the priests read from certain Buddhist sutras and then make to them an offering of money or rice.

*b.* One or more members of the family visit the temple on certain Buddhist fete-days.

*c.* Each family has a sort of shrine where the family idols and tablets are kept. To this a priest or priests are invited on certain days of the year to have a mass performed for its deceased members.

*d.* A member or members of a Buddhist family visit the temple it patronizes on certain holy days or the days on which sermons are given.

*e.* The Buddhists hold it their duty to go to hear some great priests preach.

*f.* The Buddhists often give money to the priests in aid of the support of temples and monasteries.

*g.* A fraternity or sisterhood is formed and money is collected by subscription in aid of certain monasteries or other holy places.

There are sisterhoods of many descriptions, some for the support of certain temples, some for the propagation of the doctrine of a certain sect, and others for the benefit of certain idols. Some of these sisterhoods have several scores of hundreds of members. Among them the best known are:

1. The *Narita sisterhood* for the support of the Fudo temple in Shimosa.

2. The *Seiryoji sisterhood* for the benefit of the Seiryoji, where an image of Shakamuni carved in India is enshrined.

There is, indeed, no well-known temple in the whole country but has one or more sisterhoods laboring for its benefit. There are also many ladies' associations who invite some worthy nuns on certain days of the year in order to hear their preach. The *Hokke-shiu* and *Jodo-shiu* have each a great many sisterhoods, respectively called the *Daimoku-ko* and the *Nembutsu-ko*. The larger of these communities have presidents, secretaries, managers and treasurers, and some even standing committees for the collection of subscriptions, and for the management of miscellaneous business. These officers serve out of disinterested devotion and receive no remuneration whatever. Nor is this all. They often pay the expenses of the meetings out of their own pockets. The smaller sisterhoods have no presidents. They have only managers, who perform financial as well as other duties. The money contribution of a member of a *ko*, as a religious fraternity or sisterhood is called, varies from one to four or five *sen* per month. Some *ko* have special regulations for the mutual help of its members in case of extraordinary disasters. The *Ko* people are paid special attention to by the priests, when they visit the monasteries or temples, on funeral or other occasions. All sisterhoods perform their devotional duties so peaceably as to gain the admiration of all who know them, and that without any settled laws or regulations.

## CHAPTER V.

# JAPANESE WOMEN IN DOMESTIC LIFE.

The customs of past centuries, to some extent, still govern the lives of every Japanese woman. Rules of conduct for her daily life, and for special occasions, were rigorously enforced during the Feudal Period, and to-day exist as household mandates, somewhat modified by more modern customs. One of the indispensable qualities of a woman is gentleness of voice, united with that of manner; this naturally induces grace of movement, since the condition of the mind exerts great influence upon the body. When very young the child is carefully taught by its mother and grandmother to be graceful in manner, gentle in speech, polite and benevolent. When she becomes a wife, a mother, or a grandmother these qualities continue to be imperative.

While a strict observance of ceremony is important for both sexes, it is the most important for a woman. Formerly fixed rules regulated every daily act, at present more latitude is permitted, with due regard to etiquette. To avoid all light and frivolous conversation or conduct, to reply politely, and to pay respect to superiors in age or in rank are rules which now govern the conduct of every woman. Even in the family life differences in age and in rank are strictly regarded.

The persons to be most respected by a wife are, first, the grandparents of her husband; next, his parents; next, his elder brothers and sisters; then comes the husband; lastly, his younger brothers and sisters, as they are lower in rank than herself. The sons and daughters are also ranked according to their age, and under these rules the elder must love and care for the younger, and the younger must in return be careful in speech and in behavior and must obey the elder at all times. Among the duties of a wife it is necessary for her to teach other members of the family the rules of proper etiquette and to see that they are observed, and to conceal from all strangers any family faults. As the wife has the responsibility of the family etiquette she must be careful to observe all these rules herself; she must also understand domestic matters; know how to treat and govern her servants; to assist in the education of her children and the younger brothers and sisters; cut and make dresses for all the family, and give orders for the cooking. These and all other household duties come under her charge. Although her responsibility is very great and her duties onerous, yet she must try bravely to discharge them all and please her husband by skillfully arranging household affairs, amusing her children, and keeping the family happy and peaceful.

A woman's duties keep her generally at home, but in case she has business to attend to, she goes out, first geting permission from her father, or mother-in-law, or her husband. Besides going out for business she also goes to see the plum and cherry blossoms, fleur-de-lis, and chrysanthemums in their seasons. Sometimes she attends a concert, garden party, or the theatre, and absents herself all day. So, besides the pleasure of being at home, she has also outside enjoyment.

The three periods of a woman's life may be divided into childhood, wifehood and motherhood. We will treat each of them separately.

### No. 1—Childhood.

The birth of a child is celebrated by all members of the family. If the first child be a girl it is considered very good luck. When a child is born all the relatives and intimate friends are at once informed of the event. As soon as they receive the news they go immediately to the house, taking with them some presents to show their joy. The presents are of various kinds, but consist chiefly of cotton-goods, raw silk, silk, boxes of eggs, fish, toys, wearing apparel for the baby, and *katsuobushi* (steamed and dried fish). For some days the midwife attends and waits upon the woman in childbed, bathes the child once or twice a day, puts on loose clothing, the material of which is soft. The nurse holds the infant carefully in her arms, and does not expose it to the outside air for a certain time.

The name of the child is usually given on the seventh day after its birth. It is generally chosen by its father or grandfather, but sometimes relatives or friends who hold exalted positions will choose the name. The names of girls are entirely different from those of boys, and the sound is simpler and shorter; they are mostly taken from flowers, trees, etc. The most common are " *Matsu* " (pine), " *Take* " (bamboo), " *Ume*" (plum), " *Uri*" (lily), " *Kiku*" (chrysanthemum), etc. Sometimes the names are chosen for their good meaning.

The name of a boy is sometimes an ancestral one. This is seldom given to a girl. On the thirty-first day, if a boy, and the thirty-second, if a girl, the child is carried in the arms of a nurse or servant to the temple. The baby is dressed in an exquisite manner, with the crest of the family on the back and one on each sleeve. In case the child's father is a merchant the mother goes with it to the temple, and then takes it to visit the relatives and friends, and thanks them for the presents they have sent on the occasion of its birth.

The hosts treat it kindly, and if the child be a girl, they will give her many toys.

On the day of Miyamairi it is the custom to send *sekihan* (rice, steamed with red beans, with *katsuobushi* to those who sent presents at the child's birth. *Sekihan* is put in a beautifully decorated box called *jubako*, covered with a cloth of gold brocade, or other costly material called *fukusa*. Naturally, the value of the presents differ according to the class and rank of the relatives; still the ceremony is about the same in all classes.

The methods of bringing up a child differ greatly according to the rank of its parents.

In a noble family, two or three attendants wait upon the mother, and the baby is constantly held in their arms; they walk with it, up and down in the rooms, and they never let it lie down alone until it goes to sleep at night. These attentions are continued until the child is three or four years old.

In the middle classes some hire a wet-nurse. If this is done, the first thing is to select one who has good health; the second is to choose one who is of good character, and has an agreeable personal appearance. The nurse constantly carries the baby in her arms, feeds it when it is hungry; when it sleeps she tenderly lays it on a little cushion, and lets it sleep soundly; when it wakes she takes it up again in her arms, walks with it in the room, or out in the open air, within or out of the gate, and pleases the eyes and heart of the baby. Again, some hire a maid simply to amuse the child and not to nurse it.

In the lower classes, the methods of bringing up children differ widely from those we have mentioned. Girls, from twelve to thirteen years, are hired to take charge of the children. They are called "komori." In the street, "komori" may often be seen playing together, carrying the children on their backs, and singing nursery songs which are simple and peculiar in tune. They shake the babies on their backs to keep them quiet, and the babies putting their heads on "komori's" back, comfortably go to sleep. If the family is too poor to hire "komori," the elder sisters care for the younger ones.

The clothing of a baby is made in such a way that the body and the limbs are free from compression; then, as the sleeves are broad, and the skirt long, it is very easily put on, and taken off. Thus the proper development of the body is thoroughly secured.

When the child is five or six months old, it begins to creep, and at eight or nine months, it crawls to the knees of its mother or nurse, takes hold of their dresses, and tries to walk by itself. When over a year, it can walk about in the room without any help, and seems to be exceedingly happy. .

In Japanese houses every room is matted, and as they are always thoroughly swept, and shoes are never used upon them, they are perfectly clean, and even the corners of the room are free from dust. As the Japanese people sit on these mats, eat and sleep on them, it is therefore very convenient for the children to creep, walk and play about.

When a child is 2 or 3 years old, fine straw shoes or *zori* or *geta* (wooden clogs) are tied to its little feet, and it walks around in the garden, its mother and nurse holding it by each hand.

It is now time to begin to teach it how to speak and be polite to others. It is done in this way: The mother, grandmother, aunt or nurse talk to it constantly while playing or while amusing the child with toys; or when they hush it to sleep; or whenever they have leisure they tell it some simple and amusing story of which there are many. As the story of "The battle of an ape and a crab;" that of "The boat-war between a hare and a badger;" the story of "An old man getting a prize by making the withered old leaves blossom," and many others. These are simple and amusing, so the child soon understands them, and will repeat them itself. Thus as the child grows older it gradually understands the language.

The first morning duty of a girl is to go to her parents, and kneeling before them, to say "Ohayo gozarimasu" (good morning). When she sits at the table for her meals she bows before she takes up her chop sticks, and when she finishes she makes another bow. When she goes out to school, or elsewhere, either for play or on an errand, she kneels before her mother, bows, and then goes out. On her return she does the same. When she retires for the night she bows and says "Osakie" (excuse me for retiring before you).

In case there be a visitor in the house, or she meets relatives or friends in the halls, she must bow very politely. In a family of high rank where there are numerous female servants they wait upon the guests; but in case the visitors are relatives, or familiar friends, the daughter of the family makes tea, serves wine, or rice, and waits upon them. On such occasions she must be very polite and courteous in her behavior.

Excepting in the family of a nobleman, girls are taught, not only manners, but they are carefully taught how to cook and sew. These duties must be understood by a girl before she can marry, and go to her husband's house. It is considered a disgrace not to know how to cut and make clothing, to wash it, and to know how to attend to all household duties.

The art of cooking is not learned from a regular teacher, but is learned at home by looking on, or helping the mother or servants when they are at work. Sewing is taught at school, or by the mother, aunt, or dressmaker, and every girl spends a great deal of her time in sewing.

Amusements and games for girls are numerous, as throwing a ball vertically upon the ground, and catching it on the back of the hand, or striking it with the palm of the hand. This is a game for girls of from seven to twelve or thirteen years, and is played in a garden, or in a room while singing pretty songs. The game of the bean-bag is for girls from five to ten years of age. The bag is made of pieces of silk, or crape, filled with red beans; it is about two inches square and is played somewhat like jack-stones. The number they play with is seven, or double the number; they throw and catch them with the palm or back of the right hand and pick them up with certain fingers.

This game needs good practice and is very quiet and amusing. In January the favorite game is battledore and shuttlecock. This is played by girls of all ages and is a very pretty and healthful game. Beautifully dressed girls play the game with battledores made of light colored wood (*Paullownia imperialis*) and covered with silk raised work elaborately ornamented. They stand in a group or separate themselves at equal distances, and each one tries to strike the shuttlecock in turn and send it to her neighbor. The shuttlecock is made of five small feathers variously colored, with their stems stuck into the center of a very hard seed (*celtis-muku*). When the game is played songs are sung accompanying the sound of the seed as it strikes against the battledore and thus makes a perfect harmony.

Beside these outdoor sports there are many indoor games played exclusively in January, such as: "*Sugoroku*" (backgammon), "*Irohagaruta*" (alphabetical cards), "*Uta-garuta*" (poetical cards), "*Fukubiki*" (drawing good luck, or lottery cards). There are several kinds of "*Sugoroku*," some are of geographical or biographical pictures prettily colored. The former is thus played: A die is thrown on it by turns, and all begin their journey from the same starting point; the one who first reaches the goal wins the game. "*Iroha-garuta*" consists of two sets; one set has old proverbs written on each card, beginning with one character of the alphabet. There are forty-eight of them. Another set has proverbial pictures on each card corresponding to that of the other set. Little folks play with these in various ways. One way is to scatter all the picture cards here and there on the mats. One of the players read from the reading cards in order as they come and all the others try to get the corresponding picture cards as quickly as they can. Those who pick up the most win the game. The games of the poetical cards ("*Uta-garuta*") are more complicated and of higher character than those of "*Iroha-garuta*" and are played by older boys and girls. An old poet named *Teikakiyo* chose poems of a hundred celebrated old poets and these were written or printed on cards.

Japanese poetry is composed of two parts. On one set of the cards only the second part is written; while on the other the whole poem is inscribed. The latter set is for reading. The ways of playing these cards are numerous; sometimes they are played the same way as the " Iroha-garuta." Another way is to form sides, and divide the 100 cards into equal numbers. Each person spreads his or her cards on the mats in the space assigned for them, and then tries to get the most away from his or her opponent. The side which has some cards left over is beaten. This is a most popular and exciting game, and it is so enjoyed by the players that they do not always realize when the night is far advanced.

Another game called "*Pukubiki*," (lottery game) is played in the following manner: Several strings are held by the players at the end of which some expensive or cheap, useful, or comical things are carefully hidden, until at a certain signal the strings are drawn upon. Then, what a sight! What laughter! The room resounds with acclamations of unexpected joy. Not only do relatives and friends play this game together, but even the servants are invited to take a part. It is really amusing to see a maid trotting away with a silk hat on her head, or a very pretty young lady bearing off a large basket of charcoal.

Besides these games, there is the doll's festival for girls. This takes place in March. Tiers of shelves, covered with bright red cloth are arranged in a room. On the first tier "*hina*" (dolls) are placed splendidly dressed in gold brocade, representing the Emperors and Empresses. In the tier below are placed dolls representing royal guards, imperial female attendants, fine court-boy-musicians, one singing, one playing the flute, one the drum, and the other two the large and small "*tsuzumi*" (a kind of drum). In the next row are placed various kinds of doll's furniture, as table-sets, bureaus, boxes of many kinds all made of the finest lacquer, and many kitchen utensils. Below all this is placed many kinds of sweet cakes, dried fruits and candies.

The relatives and friends are offered, by the young people of the family "*Hishimochi*" (rice cakes cut in diamond shapes), white sake (a sweet liquor made of rice and resembling milk), sweets, and other dainties, and of which the dolls are supposed to partake. This festival lasts from the 1st to the 3d. On the last day guests are invited, and a feast is provided, and partaken from the small tables prepared for the dolls.

When a girl is born in a family a new set of "*hina*" (dolls) is added, and each generation retains those of the former, as they are only used once a year. Until the later years of the Tokugawa government, girls' festivals were also celebrated in July and September, but these are now given up. Girls, in order to be learned and accomplished, also skilled in all industrial work, must go to school. So the poor, as well as the wealthy, enter the kindergarten at about three years of age, and afterwards go to the primary schools, from which they graduate at about fourteen. They then enter the schools of a higher grade. Children going to the kindergarten are accompanied by their nurses or servants, while children of the nobility generally go in carriages or jinrikshas, though some of them walk.

Obedience to parents is the chief feature of a girl's moral education. This is not only taught her at school, but her parents and superiors constantly impress it upon her mind in their every-day talk. Thus a girl learns to feel that obedience is her most important duty, and she will never disobey her parents, but will endure any hardship to cheerfully and obediently serve them. This is a custom which has been handed down from generation to generation, and there are many touching stories of filial piety which are known to all young people.

### No. 2—Wifehood.

The age at which girls enter into married life is generally from seventeen to twenty-two. When a girl is of a proper age to marry, her parents ask their friends to find some suitable match for her. Even when not asked, should there be a good match, friends will call on her parents and tell them about it. In case both parties think every condition is satisfactory, the middleman manages to have a formal meeting between the two young people. After this, if each has no aversion for the union, the bridegroom sends to the prospective bride some rich material for an *obi* (sash), or a silk *kimono* (dress), with sake and fish. In return, the bride sends her future husband silk for a *hakama* (or outside dress). This is called the *Yuino*, and is equivalent to a betrothal. These presents at the time of espousal are sent through the middleman. The middleman is, in a measure, responsible for the good faith of both parties. When the engagement is agreed upon, relatives and friends send presents of silk, *Katsuobushi*, silk-wadding, or other valuable things, as congratulations on the betrothal.

The day preceding the wedding the clothing, jewels and all the effects belonging to the bride are put in *"tansu"* (bureaus) and in long chests called *"nagamochi,"* and carried to her future home. The presents she has to give to the family are sent at the same time. These are carried by coolies in procession. The length of the procession, that is, the number of *"tansu"* or *"nagamochi,"* and trays of presents, depend upon the wealth and rank of the family. The day of the bride's entrance into her husband's house is considered of great importance.

The wedding ceremony was formerly most solemnly celebrated. Recently it has been much simplified. In very wealthy and noble families they still keep to the old style and gravely and strictly go through the whole ceremony. An abbreviated account may be interesting:

The room in which the ceremony takes place is decorated with artistically arranged flowers and hanging *"kakemono"* (pictures). These must be carefully selected. They should represent the *pine, †bamboo, ‡plum, §stork, §turtle, and any other object that denotes good luck and happiness.

---

* The *pine* is an evergreen and is lasting, and is emblematic of a faithful heart.

† The *bamboo* is also an evergreen, it endures the heavy snow, cutting wind, and does not easily break; its flexibility and enduring qualities are emblematic of an upright mind.

‡ The *plum* is beautiful and blooms under the snow.

§ The *stork* is supposed to live a thousand years, and the turtle ten thousand years, and they represent longevity.

At the marriage ceremony the bride and the bridegroom are seated opposite each other. The go-between or middleman, his wife, and sometimes one or two attendants are present. One of the latter gives to the bride one of three cups of sake, which are placed one above the other upon a small dai, or stand, used only upon wedding occasions. The bride drinks a few drops, and then it is handed to the bridegroom by the middle-man. This form is carefully observed three times with each cup, hence it is called "*San-san-kudo*," or three times three (nine cups). This ceremony over, the invited relatives and friends are introduced to the couple and all unite in partaking of a banquet.

A few days after the wedding the newly married couple go to the house of the bride's father. This is called "*Sato-gaeri*" (returning home). The relatives and friends on her side are invited and together they enjoy a sumptuous feast.

Some days after this, "*seki han*" (red bean rice), with "*katsuobushi*" (dried fish), are sent to those who gave wedding gifts. This is almost the same as at the birth of a child.

When a girl is married her most important duty is to serve and obey her husband. Foreigners who are not acquainted with our customs may perhaps imagine that a Japanese woman is a slave to her husband, but this is not the case. As the virtues of politeness and obedience are greatly cherished by our women, so a wife always respects her husband and endeavors to speak to him with modest obedience. The husband in return loves his wife and never puts an unreasonable task upon her. Besides this he leaves all household affairs entirely to her management, so her power at home almost equals that of a queen.

The management of her servants, the discipline of the house and domestic arrangements, are matters to which she must pay great attention.

In addition to her husband there are others in the household whom a wife must respect and dutifully obey. These are the father and mother-in-law. They are to be treated just as if they were her own parents. Until they become "*inkyo*" (retired) all household duties and power belong to the mother-in-law, but after her retirement these duties are transferred to the daughter-in-law. Even after their retirement the manners of the daughter-in-law towards them must remain unchanged. The daily duties of a wife are of various kinds: Purchasing articles of food, directing the cook, sending presents to people, receiving lady visitors and the friends of her husband. Among other things making dresses for herself and husband is considered the most necessary. A wife must ever be ready to serve and help her husband and also be faithful to his interests.

### No. 3—Motherhood.

If a wife is childless it is considered most unfortunate, as it will be difficult for her to retain the warm affection of her husband and the love of her father and mother-in-law. Consequently, domestic harmony is very likely to decrease and the pleasure of the home-life is greatly diminished. On the contrary, if the wife is blessed by children, she is respected and loved by all in the family. She makes her home a place of happiness and brightness and cheers up all hearts. This is because children are so lovable and are the knot that joins loving hearts to each other. As Japan is a country where the line of succession is strictly regarded and where great pride is taken in an unbroken descent, naturally great distress is felt when there is no heir for the house. A mother's love for her children is so deep that nothing can compare with it. Human nature is the same all over the world, high or low, rich or poor. The mother always has her child near her and does not permit the nurse to take it far from home, nor does she allow it to be absent long from her sight. When it laughs she embraces it; when it cries she soothes it in her arms, puts everything away for it and devotes herself entirely to its care. So she declines invitations to garden parties, concerts, or the theatre; she sacrifices all kinds of enjoyments for the sake of her dear child; neither does she regret having done so. No one thinks it strange or out of place. On the contrary, if she should go out for her own pleasure, leaving her child at home, many would say that she had but little love for her child and would therefore despise her.

The education of children, especially of girls, is left entirely with the mother; not because the father does not love them, but because the mother's cares and attentions are so thorough that he need not interfere.

Although a mother loves her children so much, still she takes heed not to spoil them. She always tries to teach them politeness and the proper manner of behavior.

It is well to bring up a child strictly but overstrictness is not always advisable, therefore when a child has done something wrong the mother reproves it seriously, but the reproof of a mother differs much from that of a father. A mother's is more tender and the child instead of flying away to escape the reproof of its mother will obediently ask her forgiveness.

The daily life of a mother is one of many duties. She must arise early, summon the servants to open the doors and prepare the breakfast; she also directs the servants to wake up the children and dress them if they are too young to do it for themselves.

After breakfast she prepares her children for school, puts together books, note books, luncheon-boxes, etc., and instructs how to bow and say *sayonara* (good-bye) before going out, to their parents and grandparents. Then it is time to attend to her husband and prepare whatever he may need to take away with him. When all is ready she goes to the *genkan* (porch) where the *jinrikisha* (carriage drawn by a man) is waiting for him, and here she bids him *sayonara*. When he has gone she puts away his clothing, and after arranging all things in an orderly manner sits down to her sewing. While her delicate fingers are busily engaged with her needle, the fish or vegetable man comes and she orders her servants what to buy. Afterwards she receives her lady visitors or transacts any business a messenger may bring her. She is careful to see that the messenger has some tea, or she provides him with dinner, or supper if it is a suitable hour.

When the children come joyfully home from school in the afternoon they go at once to their mother and say "*Tadaima*" (we have just come home). The mother welcomes them with gladness, gives them some fruit or cakes, asks them to repeat what they have learned that day and explains to them what they do not understand.

After that she amuses them by telling interesting tales. Then they go to their grandparents' room and tell them what they have done at school, and the old people will amuse them by telling stories or playing with them.

About this time she hears a jinrikiska-man call out, *"Okairi"* (returned) and her husband gets out of the jinrikisha. The mother hurries to welcome him to his home with her children and servants. She assists him in changing his dress and otherwise helps him. Then she sits near him and gives him a minute account of what has happened during his absence. This done it is time for her to order the supper.

Not long after this the house is closed for the night, but if the husband goes out in the evening it is the duty, as well as pleasure, of the wife to be awake on his return and have ready some tea and other refreshments.

# CHAPTER VI.

# JAPANESE WOMEN IN INDUSTRIAL OCCUPATIONS.

Japan is a country which possesses great advantages in its physical situation and is rich in the products of both sea and land. Its form is long and narrow and extends diagonally from southwest to northeast.

Although the whole country is in the temperate zone, half of Chishima in the north lies in the frigid zone, while the islands of Okinawa in the south are very near to the Tropic of Cancer, thus it has all climates, cold, warm, dry and wet. Accordingly in it are found the various products of the temperate, torrid and frigid regions.

From Hokkaido may be obtained seals, herring, salmon, *kombu* (a kind of sea-weed), and other marine products.

The islands of Okinawa and Ogasawara produce sweet potatoes, sugar cane, tobacco, bananas, cocoanuts, lemons and pineapples.

The country is very mountainous. In the interior chains of mountains extend from one extremity to another and level tracts of land are comparatively scarce, still the land is very fertile and productive. The warm current of the Pacific Ocean washes the southeastern shore, and the southeast wind from the tropical region brings with it a vast quantity of vapor. These together, fertilize the country and help the growth of animals and vegetables. So the soil and climate are well adapted for the production of rice, grain, silk, mulberry and timber. As there are longitudinal mountain ranges, various valuable minerals are found in great quantities. The coal region especially is very extensive and more than half of its product is exported.

The country is entirely surrounded by ocean and seas, and its coast line is indented with harbors, bays and gulfs, while numerous islands cluster near the shore. The length of the coast line, including all the islands, is estimated at more than 15,300 ri (about 45,000 miles); the main island alone has a coast line of 3,800 ri (about 9,000 miles); so there is every convenience for fishing and making salt.

As for Hokkaido, it is one of the three great fishing places of the world. Besides, it is most convenient for shipping and commerce.

As the country has such favorable physical features the climate and the soil are well suited for extensive productions, so agriculture, rearing silk-worms and fishing have been carried on from the earliest ages. These different employments were highly developed more than a thousand years ago and a good degree of civilization resulted therefrom. Grain and fruits were produced, saké and sauces were made in great quantities in those days.

The arts of sculpture and wood engraving also received much attention from skilled workmen. The grand Buddhist temple of Horinji, noted for its splendid carvings in wood, as well as the beauty of the edifice, are enough to prove both the beauty of the timber and the skill of its workmanship.

Again the great bronze statue of Buddha, fifty-four feet high, in the temple of Todaiji in Nara; the copper statues of Nikko, Gekko and Yakushi in Yakushiji, and the still older gilded weapons of copper and iron dug out of the ground show that mining, as well as the arts of casting and working in metals, were far advanced. The beautiful and delicate silk brocades and other costly materials preserved carefully in the storehouses tell us that the arts of rearing silk-worms and weaving were also greatly perfected. Besides these, many other things which show the developed state of different industries are found among the treasures carefully preserved in these same storehouses, such as mosaic work, decoration of mirrors, checker-boards of inlaid work, prayer-book cases ornamented with agate, silver, gold and tortoise-shell work, colored ivory or glass work, peculiar paintings done with paints called *Mitsudaso*, lathe work, colored earthen ware and dyed materials. There is really no limit if we attempt an enumeration. Such were some of the industries at the period when Nara was the Imperial capital, or even before that time, about 1,000 or 1,300 years ago. Since then many great improvements have taken place.

We will here add a list of the productions of the different provinces:

Honshiu.

Tokyo—Silks, cotton cloth, cotton thread, socks, round fans, colored pictures, tortoise-shell work, gold-lacquer work, brushes, wooden clogs, bamboo work, beer, wines, cigars and various kinds of paper.

Kyoto—Silks (brocade, satin, velvet, etc.), dyed stuffs, embroideries, fans, porcelain, metal work, lacquer, toys, powder, rouge, tea, etc.

Osaka—Cotton thread, socks, tobacco pipes and cases, toys, tortoise-shell work, saké, etc.

Kanagawa-Ken—Silks, cotton cloth, raw silk, preserved vegetables, different kinds of fish, etc.

Hiogo-Ken—Leather work, cotton, sauces, salt, saké, *yanagigori* (traveling box made of willow), raw silk, etc.

Niigata-Ken—Lacquer, petroleum, *sudare* (a shade made of split bamboo or reeds), silks, cotton, various kinds of fish, etc

Saitama-Ken—Cotton cloth, raw silk, etc.

Chiba-Ken—Sweet potatoes, sauces, sweet saké, fagots, charcoal, sardines, dried sardines, *katsuobushi* (dried fish), etc.

Ibaraki-Ken—Tobacco, paper, tea, silks, cotton cloth, *shimekasu* (boiled sardines, pressed in frames, dried and used as a fertilizer).

Gumma-Ken—Raw silk, silks, cotton cloth, *tanegami* (paper on which the eggs of silk worms are deposited).

Tochigi-Ken—Cotton, silks, raw silks, flax, lacquer, lathe wood, etc.

Nara-Ken—Cotton cloth, linen, lacquer, timber, *kudzu* (the "pachyrrhizus thunbergianus"), etc.

Miye-Ken—Tea, rice, grain, fish, cotton, timber, paper, pottery (*banko-yaki*), tobacco cases, umbrellas, mats, lacquer, shellfish, seaweeds, etc.

Aichi-Ken—Earthenware, saké, vinegar, fans, cotton cloth, mosaic work, etc.

Shidzuoka-Ken—Tea, paper, cotton, fish, timber, etc.

Yamanashi-Ken—Silk goods, raw silk, crystals, fruits, (grapes, pears, persimmons and chestnuts), etc.

Shiga-Ken—Oil, linen, raw silk, silks, floor mats, lime. etc.

Gifu-Ken—*Kozo* (paper mulberry, broussonetia papyrifera), mino-paper, striped cotton cloth, tea, paper lanterns, timber, raw silk, lime, etc.

Nagano-Ken—Raw silk, *tanegami*, silks, cotton cloth, linen, floor mats, timber, drugs, etc.

Miyagi-Ken — Silk goods, raw silk, flax, *katsuobushi*, oysters, shimekasu, dried beche-de-mer, and other kinds of fish, etc.

Fukushima-Ken — Raw silk, *tanegami*, lacquer, copper work, horses, etc.

Iwate-Ken—Raw silk, silk goods, linen, iron pots, fishing nets, horses, oxen, etc.

Aomori-Ken—Raw silk, silk goods, mats, oxen, horses, sea products (codfish, dried sardines, dried sea-ears, dried beche-de-mer, and different kinds of shellfish), etc.

Yamagata-Ken — Raw silk, silk goods, flax, copper work, etc.

Akita-Ken—Silk goods, lacquer, macaroni, metals (gold, silver, copper and lead), metal work, etc.

Fukui-Ken—Silk goods, linen, paper, edged-tools, etc.

Ishikawa-Ken—Earthenware (Kutani), lacquer, copper work, inlaid work of gold and silver, cotton, raw silk, silk goods, vermicelli, different kinds of fish, etc.

Toyama-Ken—Cotton, medicine, copper-casting, straw mats, different kinds of fish, etc.

Tottori-Ken—Cotton cloth, raw silk, iron, steel, etc.

Shimane-Ken—Cotton, iron, steel, wax, etc.

Okayama-Ken— Cotton cloth, floor mats, earthenware, tobacco, etc.

Hiroshima-Ken—Cotton, salt, floor mats, oysters, etc.

Yamaguchi-Ken—Salt, cotton, flax, earthenware, etc.

Wakayama-Ken — Camphor, timber, oranges, different kinds of fish, etc.

Shikoku.

Tokushima-Ken—Indigo, tobacco, salt, etc.

Kagawa-Ken—Sugar, salt, stones, etc.

Ehime-Ken—Wax, salt, sauce, sugar, paper, etc.

Kochi-Ken—Paper, *katsuobushi*, coral, etc.

Kiushiu.

Nagasaki-Ken—Wax, coal, lacquer, tortoise-shell work, tobacco, earthenware, etc.

Fukuoka-Ken—Wax, silks, cotton cloth, candles, sake, camphor, floor mats, etc.

Oita-Ken—Floor mats, figured mats, camphor, etc.

Saga-Ken—Camphor, wax, tobacco, earthenware, paper, etc.

Kumamoto-Ken—Paper, flax, floor mats, cotton cloth, etc.

Miyazaki-Ken—Paper, timber, camphor, different kinds of fish.

Kagoshima-Ken—Camphor, sugar, fish, cotton cloth, tobacco, earthenware, etc.

Okinawa-Ken-(Liu choo)—*Jofu* (grass cloth of the finest quality), sugar, floor mats, lacquer, pongee, etc.

Hokkaido-(Yezo)—Sea products (salmon, cod, *kombu*, herring, sardines, whales, seals, dried beche-de-mer, etc.), linen, coal, sulphur and timber.

These are only the most famous products, but it may be seen from this list that there is a great variety.

In farming, fishing, cutting timber and in all kinds of industries women always do a share of the work, and we may positively assert that one-third of all the above enumerated products are obtained by their labor.

The population of the empire on the 31st of December, 1890, the twenty-third year of Meiji, was estimated at 40,453,461. Males, 20,431,097; females, 20,022,364.

The Department of Agriculture and Commerce investigated the exact number of men and women engaged in different occupations. The result was as follows:

|  |  |  |
|---|---|---|
| In Agriculture, - | Males, | 11,400,008 |
|  | Females. | 10,948,053 |
|  | Total. | 22,348,061 |
| In different industries, | Males, | 1,017,200 |
|  | Females, | 940,649 |
|  | Total. | 1.957.849 |

|  |  | Males, | 2,113,634 |
|---|---|---|---|
| In Commerce, | | Females, | 1,878,098 |
|  | | Total, | 3,991,732 |
| Miscellaneous Business, | | Males, | 2,591,585 |
|  | | Females, | 2,749,945 |
|  | | Total, | 5,341,530 |

It is to be much regretted there are so few authentic records of the work done by women in ancient times. The lives of a few women have been written, but they were mostly celebrated for their skill in playing on different instruments, or in composing poetry; very few names are mentioned of women who were engaged in productive employments, and these few are inaccurate; still it is an undisputed fact that women have done a great part of the work of rearing silk worms, weaving and other important industries for more than 2,000 years.

As we shall write something of agriculture, forestry, marine productions, different industries and commerce in regular order, we shall describe work done by women. We shall also give historical data, as well as the present condition of various productive occupations in the different provinces of the empire.

### Agriculture.

#### FORESTRY.

Agriculture is the source of the wealth of our country. Rice and grain are used for our daily food, so the work of the farmer has always been regarded as very important, and every means has been taken to encourage it. Although the surface of the country is generally mountainous, its mountain sides, as well as its valleys and plains, are ploughed and cultivated. The land owned amounts to 13,794,361 tan, about 2,751,526 *tan* and 7 *ho* being in rice fields and 2,291,127 *tan* and 8 *ho* being in small farms. (1 *tan*=10,800 sq. ft. 1 *ho*=36 sq. ft.)

The chief products for food are rice, barley, wheat, buck-wheat, millet, beans, small red beans, indian corn, sweet potatoes, greens, fruits, etc. The materials manufactured are cotton, flax, sugar cane, tobacco, indigo, rape-seed, oil, wax, lacquer, *gampi* (a kind of thin paper Wickstroemia canescens), edgeworthia papyrifera, *kozo*, etc.

The chief articles of export are tea, silk and lacquer. Rearing silk worms is the occupation of the peasants in Shinano, Kotsuke, Iwashiro, Musashi and other districts. The yearly production of cocoons is 1,115,000 *koku* (1 *koku*= bushels, 5,555); that of *tanegami* from 230,000 to 240,000 sheets; raw silk from 800,000 to 1,000,000 *kwan* (1 *kwan*= lbs., 8,282); floss silk and waste silk, each 40,000 to 50,000 kwan.

Tea is grown in every district except in Hokkaido. The amount of tea exported in the twenty-third year of Meiji (1890) was 37,250,720 *kin* (1 *kin*=1⅓ lb.), and its value about 6,326,881 yen.

More than half of the women of the country are employed in agriculture. In the spring, when the snow still lies deep on the ground, they clean the rice from the hulls facing the cold north wind, or they manure the mulberry trees, tea and the *kozo* plants.

From the 18th of March they are busy sowing the seeds of different kinds of beans and other vegetables, grafting trees, etc. When it is warmer and the shoots of rice begin to grow, it is time to plough, cultivate the fields and plant other seeds and trees.

On the 2d of May the silk worms grow to their full size and eat great quantities of mulberry leaves, then is the time when those who are engaged in rearing silk worms find it hard to rest, either by day or night.

In June the shoots of rice are separated, the winter wheat is reaped, seeds are sown, and this is the busiest season for the farmer.

When summer comes the rice fields must be irrigated and weeded. This is also the season in which to cut and dry tobacco and indigo leaves.

In September, when the soft autumn coolness begins to be felt and everything is ripe, the rice harvest begins; ploughing also is done, and wheat is sown and transplanted.

In November, all the farm work is finished, but coverings for trees must be prepared to protect them from the frost and wood must be cut for fuel.

Large numbers of women are engaged in these labors during the entire year.

## HISTORICAL ACCOUNT OF AGRICULTURE.

As our country is fertile and well adapted for the growth of five cereals (wheat, rice, millet, beans and sorghum), the art of cultivation was known from the earliest ages.

Formerly linen was largely used for clothing, and the art of rearing silk worms was practiced by women from early times, indeed the Empresses themselves were often known to rear worms and engage in weaving. The Emperor Sujin (B. C. 97-30) made new tax laws. The tax paid by a man was called *Uhazu-no-mitsugi*, and that of a woman was called *Tana-sue-no-mitsugi*. *Uhazu-no-mitsugi* means "an offering of deer horns, skins of bears and other animals killed by himself." *Tana-sue-no-mitsugi* means "an offering of silk or cloth woven by the woman." Thus it appears that women had an equal share in the daily industry at a very remote period.

At the time of the Emperor Ojin (A. D. 283), Uzuki, Prince of Kudara (a province of Corea), came to Japan with emigrants from 127 other provinces. These people were skillful in rearing silk worms and in weaving. The Emperor Yuriaku (457-479) encouraged this industry and ordered Sugaru, an official, to collect the eggs of silk worms for his Empress "Kusaka-no Hata-hime," and for her to feed the worms and attend to all the work herself. From this time this became a most important occupation for women.

During the reign of the Emperor Kotoku (A. D. 645) a census was taken so that the accurate number of the population was known; the land was surveyed and a register made of all cultivated lands, also new rules regarding the taxes were proclaimed. This was called *Handen*, that is, two *tan* of land was given to a man, and two-thirds of two *tan* given to a woman, and both were to pay their taxes to the government in work. *Uhazu-no-mitsugi* and *Tana-sue-no-mitsugi* were now abolished, but the women had to cultivate a certain amount of land which was assigned to them and also weave silk or linen as before.

From the time of the Emperor Saga to the Emperors Junwa, Ninmei, Buntoku, Seiwa and Koko (ninth century) they all made great efforts to improve agriculture; ordering the governor of each province to go himself and encourage the farmers to improve ponds and water courses, and thus increase irrigation, and to also do all possible to aid in the fertilizing of the land. They often lessened the taxes, fed the people and helped their wants in many ways.

When the Fujiwara family grasped the power dissipation, luxury and idleness were the order of the day, and the discipline of the government was lessened. The result was, discontented men rose in mobs, collecting others in different parts of the country, and defied the officials, robbed the helpless people and prevented the farmer from working peacefully in his fields. Thus many of the farmers lost the seasons for rearing silk-worms or cultivating the soil. So the rice fields and the farms lay waste. This frequently happened, especially in the time of *Hogen* and *Heiji* (1156-1159). The war between the two houses, *Genji* and *Heike*, gave no peace to the farmers, and they were obliged to take their families and property and fly to the mountains. Their rice fields and farms were trampled over by war horses, or, if they fortunately escaped that calamity, they could not evade the heavy taxes which they were obliged to pay to the governor of the province for the expenses of the war. The sufferings of the farmers were extremely great.

When *Yoritomo*, the great general, established a temporary government and a member of the *Hojo* house became the Prime Minister (1220) but little peace was obtained. *Yasutoki* and *Tokiyori* of the *Hojo* house frequently relieved the people when suffering from want, and reprimanded the lords of the provinces for their tyrannical conduct. For a while the farmers felt as if they might recover from their losses but this hope did not last long. The latter part of the *Kamakura* government (1331) was filled with the horrors of civil war between the houses of the North and the South, both having a rightful claim to the throne of Japan.

Then the power of the temporary government passed to the *Ashikaga* family and afterwards to the *Toyotomi* family. During an interval of 300 years the country was constantly in a state of confusion and disturbance and the people could not engage in peaceful occupations. The women were in a very miserable condition during this war-like period. The power of the whole empire lay in the force of arms, and for anyone without a name, without an education, but skillful in the art of war there was an opportunity to rise at once to a great military career. Naturally all persons regarded military service with great respect. Men could do as they liked but women were kept in a state of submission, and while some took charge of the most difficult household labors during the absence of their husbands many others entered into the service of houses of higher rank.

Each military man, or *samurai* (knight), served his feudal lord generation after generation. As the heir of the house was limited to the male sex, should the heir die the allowance from the lord was cut off; thus a greater respect was felt for men than for women and this had the effect of making the latter weak-minded and without courage. This war-like condition of the country thus made a remarkable change in the state and occupations of women.

The seeds of the tea plant came to Japan in the time of the *Fujiwara* family, but for many years tea was not much used. At the beginning of the *Kamakura* government (1190) *Eisei*, the founder of the *Zenshu* (one of the religious sects), brought the tea again from So (China), and it gradually came into general use. When the *Ashikaga* Shogun, *Higashiyama* favored the *"Cha-no-yu"* it became very fashionable and it now seems that tea is an indispensable beverage.

The cotton seed was known in the time of the *Fujiwara* family, but afterwards it went entirely out of cultivation. In the year 1592 it was planted for the second time and soon a great amount of cotton cloth was woven, and took the place of silk and linen for wearing apparel. Spinning and weaving cotton and picking tea leaves became suitable occupations for women and they were constantly employed in these labors.

When the government of the country fell into the hands of the *Tokugawa* family in 1603, the great Shogun *Iyeyasu*, practiced the greatest economy; he forbade all luxury and encouraged farming. When out hunting he would go about among the people to study their condition. Accordingly the lords and governors of different provinces became more merciful to the farmers and encouraged agriculture; thus with peace the state of both men and women became more flourishing.

Proclamations were issued from the temporary government of the *Bakufu*, in which there were many laws respecting the occupations of women.   A few examples will suffice.

The following is an extract from a proclamation issued by the temporary government of the *Bakufu* in the second year of *Heian*, 1649:   (The first part is omitted.)

" The husband and wife must work together for their mutual benefit, the man in farming and the woman in spinning and weaving till late in the evening.   If a wife neglects her husband, drinks too much tea, or spends her time in pleasure, or sight seeing, then, although she may be handsome, her husband may divorce her; but in case they have many children, or if she has done some meritorious service for him in time past it will make a difference.   On the other hand if she tries to work for the good of her husband's house she must be treated with much kindness, etc."

Here is another example.   This is from the manuscript of an announcement issued by the governor of Tosa Province, named *Nonaka Denemon:*   (The first part is omitted.)

"Daughters of peasants from 10 to 16 years of age must have some work assigned them according to their age and ability."

Again it says:

"The children of peasants from the age of 8 or 9 must learn some kind of occupation."

(Here an omission.)

"In the fishing districts boys and girls must be taught various methods in regard to fishing.   When a boy reaches 8 or 9 years he must learn to handle the oars, make nets or other fishing tackle. . These may differ somewhat according to the different districts.   Girls must learn to spin flax and do other kinds of women's work.   When they are 15 or 16 years old they must decide how much work they can do during the month and make it known to the owners of houses or to the elders of the place, and then they must go together to the temple of the family gods, and register a report of their work in the proper book, etc."

These public notices show how much work was done by women in those days, and even now much the same rules are observed.   Since the country has been opened to foreign commerce some alterations have taken place, but in regard to agriculture or forestry we see no remarkable change except that business has greatly increased.   Idle girls have been encouraged to work and earn money by rearing silk worms, and picking tea leaves. Indeed, since these two products have made so great an item in the exports to foreign countries women have had more chance to earn their living than ever before.

## Present Condition of the Provinces.

The largest plain in Japan is found by the shore of the *Ishi-kari* River in *Hokkaido;* next is the plain of *Kwanto;* then that between Mino and Owari, and one in the neighborhood of Chikugo River; and all the land excepting the bare, rugged mountains and sandy regions, is thoroughly cultivated and the larger part of it is taken up in rice fields. The provinces of Musashi, Ise, Hitachi, Iwashiro, Rikuzen, Ugo, Echigo, Owari, Mino, Omi, Hoki, Idzu, Chikuzen, Chikugo, Higo and Hizen are the richest in producing rice. The amount of rice produced annually in these provinces reaches a total of 30,000,000 to 40,000,000 Koku. (1 Koku=5, 13 bu.)

Women are engaged in the cultivation of the rice fields and it is the most important work in which they can be employed. They sow the seeds early in the spring and wait until the warm rains have caused them to sprout, then with much singing and merry laughter they are transplanted into regular rows. When the shoots are a little grown, the fields are carefully weeded. In the hot summer days when there are no ponds or rivers near the fields, water must be carried from morning until night to irrigate the growing plants. When the harvest time comes women cut the rice, dry, thresh and whiten it. Then it is ready for market. During these busy days the women have also to cultivate other grains and vegetables, rear silk worms, dry tea leaves. In the evening they grind meal and spin thread, etc.

The provinces of Shinano, Kotsuke, Iwashiro and Musashi are noted for silk; and Uji of Yamashiro, Shigara of Omi, Sayama of Musashi, and the provinces of Ise and Mino are the districts best suited for the growth of the tea plant. During the silk and tea seasons not only are the women of the place engaged, but many from different districts come to be hired. Thus the locality becomes very lively for a certain time. Singing, talking and laughing are heard in every house. The wages are from 15-25 sen a day during the season.

During the tea season in the districts of Shidzuoka women come in parties of 200 or 300 to be hired. They come from Idzu, Sagami and other provinces. When their work is done they return to their homes in better condition than when they left. They travel home in new suits of summer clothes, and carry new parasols, and seem to be very gay and happy. In Yamato, Kii, Suruga, Towtowmi, Idzu, Shinano and other provinces where the forest trees propagate rapidly, women plant the young shoots and take charge of them.

### The Fishing Industry.

Our most important products are obtained from the sea, so the net and line are essential implements for increasing the wealth of the country. Although many countries are surrounded by water, are rich in rivers and lakes, no other country has the same advantages that we have.

The east, south and west coasts, facing the seas, are indented with bays and capes. As the climate is temperate, fish, shellfish and seaweeds of various kinds grow abundantly.

The northern shore is washed by the waters of the Arctic Ocean which is filled with fish, and abounds in different kinds of sea animals. In the interior of the country rivers run in various directions; lakes and marshes are scattered here and there, so the products of fresh matter are also abundant. Where so many varieties of fish and other sea products abound, it is no wonder that with a few vegetables fish has been the almost invariable food of the people, and even the manure for rice (our "staff of life") is prepared from dried fish.

The principal sea products at present are sardines, herring, *katsuo*, cuttlefish, codfish, salmon, beche-de-mer, seaweeds, etc. There are sixty varieties of sea products of which the value is estimated at over 10,000 yen a year. The total value of the sea products of the twenty-first year of Meiji (1888) is as follows: Herring, 4,323,176 yen; sardines, 2,325,840 yen; katsuo, 1,617,515 yen. The sum total of these with other fish were 19,369,480 yen.

The principal exports now are cuttlefish, seaweeds, beche-de-mer, dried sea ear, crabs, etc. These are sent chiefly to China.

From the earliest ages the people of Japan have used fish for food, although sometimes the flesh of venison and of birds has been eaten. In later years, however, flesh was not much used, and fish only was used at each meal, and even those who lived in inland towns would send to purchase fish from places near the seacoast.

In "*Yengishiki*" (books of ceremonies written in the year of *Yengi* A. D. 927) we find the names of fish and other sea products which were brought from different provinces to the Imperial Culinary Department as tribute. These were for the daily use of the Imperial household, or for offerings to the gods on holidays. The following is a list of the various articles brought and the places from whence they came:

Katsuo, from Shima, Suruga, Sagami, Awa, Kii, Idzu, Tosa, Bungo and Awa. Cuttlefish, from Wakasa, Tango, Aki, Idzumo, Chikuzen and Buzen. Large sardines, from Bitchiu, Bingo, Kii and Sanuki. Hishoko sardines, from Bitchiu, Aki and Suwo. Dried beche-de-mer, from Oki, Higo, Wakasa, Chikuzen, Shima, Hizen and Noto. Oshiayu, from Kii, Bizen, Bitchiu, Bingo, Buzen, Hizen, Higo, Tosa, etc. Tai (serranus Marginalis), from Idzumi, Shima, Ise, Sanuki, Wakasa, etc. Salmon, from Echigo, Echizen, Tamba, etc. Sea ear, from Shima, Awa, Hizen, Higo, Chikuzen, etc. Hiuwo, from Yamashiro and Omi. Suzuki, from Yamashiro. Aji, from Idzumi. Carp, from Mino. Trout, ameno uwo and funa, from Omi. Hara-aka (red breast), from Higo and Chikugo. Mackerel, from Iyo, Tosa, Suwa and Noto. Oysters, from Ise and Higo. Dried cuttlefish, from Higo and Sanuki. Dried turtle (terrapin), from Yamato. Crabs, from Owari. Different kinds of dried fish, from Owari, Mikawa, Kaga and other provinces. And many kinds of seaweeds.

We thus see that many sea products were then used for food and were obtained from many provinces.

From the last part of the reign of the *Fujiwara* family to the time of the *Kamakura* government the dishes used at court or at the tables of the Ministers of State consisted of carp, tai, sea ear, cuttlefish, crabs, trout, beche-de-mer, lobster, oyster, different kinds of shellfish and seaweeds.

In 1080 *Shirakawa Tenno* forbade anyone to take the life of any living creature, he ordered more than 8,800 fishing nets to be burned, put a stop to the tribute of fish, and he himself abstained entirely from eating either fish or meat. This he did because he was an ardent believer in Buddhism. This state of feeling did not last long.

Passing from the *Ashigaga* reign to the peaceful days of the *Tokugawa*, the amount of sea products increased rapidly, especially from the year *"Anei"* to *"Bunsei,"* as the learned men talked so much of the importance of protecting and encouraging the fisheries that the governors of different districts understood the need of better protective laws, and great improvements were made.

In the early part of "Meiji" old customs and laws were abandoned, every variety of fish was caught without limit and the sea products were almost exterminated. Fortunately this danger was soon realized and protective laws were again reinstated.

Fishing with line and hook and by casting nets is done mostly by men, but cutting seaweeds, carrying salt water to manufacture salt, diving into the sea for sea ears and salting and drying fish is done mostly by women.

### THE PRESENT CONDITION OF FISHERIES IN DIFFERENT PROVINCES.

Among the sea products, sardines, herring and *katsuo* are the principal varieties of fish and are the most abundant. Sardines are caught everywhere on the eastern coast, but the best place is *Kujukuri*. *Kujukuri* (or ninety-nine ri) has a coast line of twenty-five ri, extending from *Nagasagori* in *Kazusa* province to the promontory of *Inuboe, Shimotsuke* province. The whole length of the coast the water is very shoal, and when the sea is calm it is a most convenient place for casting nets. There are 40,000 inhabitants and more than 3,000 owners of nets in this fishing village. Men and women make their living by this occupation. In May and June, when it is the fishing season, the net profit of every village is over 1,000 yen.

During the summer months the seashore presents an animated view. Men running hither and thither, casting and drawing nets, and women carrying fish home to dry. In Hokkaido or on the Oshiu coast the same scene occurs at the herring season. Men, as well as women, go there from Iwate Fukushima, Aomori and other districts to earn money.

On the coast of Tosa, Satsuma, Kii, Isé, Shima, Sagami, Awa, Chikuzen and other provinces are found great quantities of *Katsuo*. The men catch the fish and the women stay at home and are busily engaged in making *katsuo-bushi*. One of the most remarkable occupations of the women of certain districts is that of diving into the sea for "sea ear" and various kinds of seaweeds. Women employed in this occupation are called "*Ama*."

On the coast of Ise, Shima, Noto, Wakasa and Oshiu there are many "*Ama*." They dive into the sea to the depth of about forty fathoms, search under the water, holding their breath for four or five minutes. They take with them a kind of chisel, with which they cut off the membrane holding the "sea ear" to the rock. As to the seaweeds they are cut off from the rocks, and floating to the surface are easily collected.

The most dangerous work is that of collecting "*tokoroten*" (a seaweed) in April, May, August and September, when the weeds are torn from the rocks by the force of the waves. "*Ama*," without the least fear of the storm, go out in parties to pick up these weeds.

Each "*Ama*" covering her head with a white cloth and tying a tub about her waist, throws herself into the angry waves and collects the weeds with a net called "*totta*." This is indeed a most exciting scene; it is like a battle, each one trying to get ahead of her neighbor in the quantity of weeds collected; it is likewise a very dangerous occupation and often some of the women are thrown against the rocks and are badly bruised. So a doctor from each village is always present and cares for those who are injured by any accident. Of these "*Ama*" each one earns as much as five or six yen on a stormy day. When their work is done the women of the whole village assemble and make a great feast to which all are invited.

In places where the women do the most active work the rights of the household belong to them. They have all the finances in their hands and make all the bargains relating to their work. When the women go out to their special labors their husbands or any other man at home does the cooking, washing, and even cares for the children.

As for the men, they are generally inactive, lazy, and willingly enough perform their unusual services. When they have leisure they amuse themselves with singing or playing checks, etc.

In these districts women are more respected than men, and when a girl is born she is welcomed joyfully by the whole family. She is brought up with the greatest care, but if the child is a boy he is sent away from home to be brought up by strangers. His birth is considered a disappointment for his parents.

## Other kinds of Industries.

The industry of our country is the result of constant practice for 2,000 years. Both delicate taste and skilled handiwork are very remarkable.

Silk spinning and weaving, embroidery, raised work, paper work, bamboo work, and many other things are largely done by women. Among the various articles exported to foreign countries the most important are the result of women's work. These are silk, the yearly production of which amounts to over a million *kwan*; silk goods of over forty million *tan*, silk handerchiefs, embroidered goods and many other ornamental things.

### HISTORICAL ACCOUNT OF THESE INDUSTRIES.

The arts of spinning and weaving were carried on extensively from the earliest ages. The oldest fabrics remaining are some woven at the time of the Emperor *Suigo*, A. D. 600. Only a few pieces have escaped the ravages of time. Those woven at the time of the *Nara* court in the eighth century are still well preserved. Brocade, silk damask and other fabrics were so exquisitely woven, the figures were so artistic and the coloring so beautiful, that silks woven in later years cannot enter into comparison. A few specimens of these beautiful brocades are carefully preserved in the storehouse of *Shozoin* (a storehouse in which precious antiques are kept), at

*Nanto*, and there are some others in the *Horiuji* temple. Besides weaving, women excelled in the art of dyeing silk. "*Rokitsu*" means the printing of flowers on silk and other fabrics with wax. "*Rokitsu*" is done in the following manner: A wooden board is carved with different designs of flowers, birds, etc., and the designs are then covered with wax. The silk web is then laid between two boards, the second one being smooth, and dipped into a dye. The parts left undyed, between the boards, are afterwards tastefully painted with different colors, such as light purple, dark green, scarlet, light yellow, etc.

Although the origin of weaving and dyeing in these methods is not known the term "Shibori" or "Ufuhata" seems to have been known as far back as the reign of the Empress Jingo (200 A. D.).

At the time of the *Nara* court these materials were largely used for wearing apparel, also for small carpets or rugs. Specimens of these are still seen in the storehouse of *Shozoin* and at other places. Embroidery was done most skillfully by the women of those times, and specimens are still preserved in a convent attached to the *Horiuji* temple at *Yamato*.

An embroidered "*Mandara* of *Tenjukoku*" finished in the year A. D. 623 was the work of a maid of *Tachibana no Tai-fujin*. She did this by the order of her mistress. "*Mandara*" is a picture representing men and women worshiping Buddha in Paradise.

Another "*mandara*" embroidered by *Chujohime*, finished in the year 676, is kept in the *Taema-dera* temple in *Yamoto*. *Chujohime* was a daughter of Udaijin (minister) *Toyonari*. She became a nun in *Taema-dera* convent during the year of *Tempei-hojo*. She devoted her time to embroidering a "mandara," more than fifteen feet long, with the delicate fibers of lotus stalks. Paradise was most delicately and wonderfully represented; unfortunately only a small piece of it is still preserved.

The Empress *Danrin* made a good many banners and embroidered vestments, and sent a priest named *Egaku* to China to present them to the high priests in different temples in that country. As these were not embroidered by professional artists it proves that amateurs had great skill in such work.

At the time of the *Fujiwara* government, from the ninth to the eleventh century, the people of high rank were given up to idleness and luxury, and spent their time mostly in composing poetry, playing on musical instruments and in dancing. They competed with each other in obtaining magnificent clothing and in securing the finest ·furniture, ornaments and norimonos (Sedan chairs). These latter were profusely ornamented with brocade and silk damask, and also inlaid with gold and silver and sometimes precious stones.

While the nobility were thus indulging themselves in indolence and merriment, the common people worked hard to supply the demand of the upper classes for these elegancies.

During the period of *Gengi* and *Heike* (the twelfth century) luxury reached its highest point, and the ladies of the court amused their weary hours with painting and making *hana-musubi* (making different kinds of knots of silk cords for ornaments). A prayer roll copied by the *Heike* family is preserved to this day in the storehouse of the *Itsuku-shima*. This was beautifully done and was offered to the god of the temple. It is illuminated so exquisitely that nothing can compare with it in the country. The illustrations are said to have been the work of *Kiyomori's* daughters A. D. 1160. From the time of the *Kamakura* court to the time of the *Ashikaga* family the country was in a state of great disturbance, and all kinds of industries were neglected. Among others the art of weaving fell into a state of great desuetude, compared with its condition under Imperial reigns.

There is a roll of painting called "71 *Shokunin Zukushi-rita awase*" (seventy-one workmen with poems), done by a noted artist named *Tosa Mitsunobu*, at the time of *Higashi-yama* Shogun. It represents different kinds of industries and the various conditions of the workmen. The women are represented as weaving, making saké, twisting silk cords, sewing on *kimonos* (dresses), stamping figures on cloth or paper, dyeing, etc.

From the time of the *Tokugawa* Shoguns the country was in a peaceful state and the population increased year by year;

the demand for various articles increased in proportion and the laboring classes became more prosperous.

Cotton goods, which were in general use by the common people, silk damask, satin, brocade and other materials were woven at *Kiriu, Hino* and other places about the year 1730.

Before that time all silk fabrics were woven exclusively at *Nishijin* in Kioto. Now *"Ukiori"* comes from Akita and *Sukiaya* from Echigo. The skilled weavers of Hakata of Chikuzen were removed to Kiriu and Hachioji, and silk crape is now woven at Gifu, Mino, Nagahama of Omi, Muneyama of Tanabe and Ashikaga of Shimotsuke.

Women of different provinces have also been famous for their skill in making pottery and in gold work. A few examples may be of interest: *Kane*, a daugher of Yokota Somin, and *Tsune*, a daughter of Inagawa Riokoku, were noted for their skill in gold work; and *Hamejo* of Nagasaki acquired a great name for her skill in casting.

*Yokoya Sowmin* was a famous carver who lived in Yedo (Tokio) during the period of Genroku, A. D. 1700. He obtained the first sketches of his work from the noted artists, *Kano Tanyu* and *Hanabusa Itcho,* and made the first carvings in groups. He also invented *"Keboyi"* (carving as fine and delicate as a hair).

Inagawa Riokoku, a pupil of Yanagawa Naomasa, imitated the style of Sowmin. He was especially skilled in sketching designs to be dyed on *Nanako* (a soft silk). His daughter *Tetsu* learned the art from her father and was equally celebrated for her skill. Dyeing figures upon *"Nanako"* is delicately done by the slender fingers of women, though men often get the credit of it.

*Hamejo* was a native of Nagasaki. Her father was engaged in the business of casting. Having no son he taught the secret of smelting metals to his daughter. *Hamejo* was very clever and prolific in ideas. In making delicate figures in colored copper her work was not equaled by anyone, and her name was known far and wide.

During the year of Eisei (the first part of the sixteenth century) a Chinese named *Ameya* became a citizen of Japan and lived in Keishi (Kioto). He changed his name to *Sokei* and made a peculiar kind of earthenware, which was the origin of *Rakuyaki*. After his death his widow became a nun (*ama*), and having learned the art from her husband, began making pottery, and the ware she made was called *Amayaki*.

In Kioto and other places there are many women who employ themselves in making both *Rakuyaki* and *Amayaki*, producing beautiful tea sets and many ornamental articles.

## PRESENT CONDITION OF INDUSTRIES IN DIFFERENT PROVINCES.

Various articles belonging to the "fine arts" are made in all of the principal cities of Japan. Kioto is celebrated for the manufacture of silk brocade, silk damask and velvet, also "*Shuchin*" (silk specially designed for *obis*), different kinds of gold brocade *Yuzenzome* (goods dyed in various colors), embroidery, raised work, artificial flowers, pottery, lacquer work, copper work, fans, etc.

Tokyo is noted for colored printing, round fans, small books, lacquer work, earthenware, mosaic work, gold and tortoise shell work, etc.

Nagoya is famous for mosaic work and earthenware, and Kanazawa for earthenware, copper work and inlaid work of gold and silver. Women are constantly employed in all these productions belonging to the fine arts. The women of Kyoto are famous for the skill of their handiwork and great varieties of ornamental things are made by ladies of nobility; these have a peculiar delicacy and beauty, as the art of making them has been handed down from ancient work done for pleasure by the ladies of the palace or in the houses of the nobility.

The embroidered handkerchiefs which are exported by the thousands are largely done by women.

In the cities are large rooms where they work together, and often thousands are engaged in the work. A large house in Sendai, Miyagi-Ken, others at Fukui, Fukui-Ken, Uji and Yamada of Miye-Ken, are in the most flourishing condition. Besides these workrooms women do much of this work at their own homes.

In Arita of Hizen many women are engaged in painting on earthenware. Some artists employ several women to assist them and those who are clever can make a good living.

The most important employments of women are silk spinning and weaving. Gumma, Tochigi, Fukushina, Saitama, Kanagawa, Nagano, Miyagi, Iwate, Yamagata, Yamanashi, Shiga, Gifu and other Ken are the silk districts.

The women of these districts work at their own homes or in the silk factories.

In the little town of Suwa in Shinshiu there are more than forty silk factories and several hundred women are employed in them. Girls earn more in the factories than they can earn when hired as servants, so in the vicinity of the factories it is frequently difficult to get domestics for household labors. Sometimes men are hired in the place of women or families send to other provinces for servants.

Kofu of Yamanashi, Uyeda and Suwa of Shinano have theaters and other places of amusement. These are almost empty on working days, but on holidays they are filled with thousands of women whose presence more than repay the loss felt during the working days; this one fact shows the flourishing condition of the industry of women.

Some kinds of cloth have been famous from the most ancient times as: *Nishijin ori* (cloth) of Kioto; bleached cotton of Yamato, of Nagahama; crapes and mosquito netting of Omi; *Uyeaa ori* of Shinshiu; *Matsuzaka cotton* of Ise; *Kai-silk* of Kai, *Choshi-chijima* (a kind of corrugated cloth); and *Yuki tsumugi* (pongee), of Shimosa; *Chichibu silk* of Musashi *Sendahira* of Rikuzen; *Nambu ori* of Rikuchiu; silk goods of Kotsuke; *Ashikaga silk* of Shimotsuke; *Yonezawa ori* of Ugo; *Akita ori* of Uzen, *Echigo Chijimi* of Echigo; *Hosho tsumugi* of Etchiu; *Kaga silk* of Kaga; *Unsai ori* of Mimasaka; hemp canvas of Harima; *Hakata ori* of Chikuzen; *Kokura ori* of Buzen; *Kasuri* of Satsuma; *Riu-kiu tsumugi*, and cloth woven of the plaintain fibers of the Loochu islands; *Hachijo tsumugi* of Hachijo island; and cotton from every part of the country.

In later years *futako* cotton, *Ichiraku, Hattan, Gasuori* and other goods have been woven in the vicinity of Yokohama (Hachioji is the principal place). Various kinds of cotton flannel are also woven at Kishiu and Osaka.

The amount of silk goods from the northeastern provinces and the different provinces of the Nakasendo has greatly increased, and new materials of various kinds are made every year. The methods of weaving, the rate of women's wages, customs, habits, etc., differ somewhat in different provinces.

In Kodzuke and Shimotsuke all the inhabitants are engaged in weaving. In every house is a loom; there are also places called "*Oriya*" (factories) where many women are hired to weave together. In these districts girls 6 or 7 years of age are sent to the "*Oriya*" as apprentices. Their term is for five years. Ten yen is given to their fathers or brothers at the time the contract is made. During these five years the apprentices are fed and clothed by their masters. When the term of contract is over they will receive wages of about 25 sen each day, if their skill is worth that amount. Among these girls are two good habits: one is they give the wages they receive to their parents, brothers or husbands, not wasting their money as freely as is done in some other districts. Girls here do not need to make provision for their wedding portions as do the girls of other places, so they do not hoard up their money. They apply themselves diligently to their work and try to become skilled because skill in weaving is a good marriage portion, and those who possess it are sought for by wealthy families. These customs contribute greatly to the flourishing state of these provinces.

The women weavers are generally very industrious. They rise with the sun and begin their work, never leaving the looms during the day, and the evenings they usually spend in spinning.

When a girl reaches the age of 7 or 8 years she is made to take care of the younger children, and at the same time she helps in weaving and other things.

Weaving mats, making paper toys and all articles used for the toilet is the work of women. Mats are manufactured in Bungo, Riukiu, Buzen, Chikuzen, Satsuma, Higo and other provinces of Kiushiu; also are brought from Bingo, Aki, Suwo, Omi, Mino, Shinano, etc.

The floors of our houses are covered with mats that are woven from the stalks of rushes called *yi*, and the demand for them is very great.

The mats are sewed to frames made of straw; the frames are about 2½ inches thick, 3 feet wide and 6 feet long.

Preparing the rushes for the mats, making flaxen thread with which to weave them, and much of the weaving itself is all done by women.

## PAPER MANUFACTURES.

The amount of paper manufactured in different parts of the country is enormous. Chiugoku, Shikoku and Kiushiu have each a large paper factory.

There are some differences in the details of the manufacture of paper, varying with the locality and the nature of the plant, but the general method employed is as follows: The *Koso* plants (Broussonetia papyrifera) are cut into lengths of about three feet and are then steamed in a large boiler; the bark is peeled off and boiled in lye, and after keeping it in water for some time is well pounded; then this pulp is mixed with a certain amount of diluted mucilage made from the root of the "*tororo*" (Hibiscus) and is steeped in a wooden tank. When it has remained long enough it is spread out into sheets by means of a sieve. As soon as the water has drained off, each sheet, with the aid of a straw brush, is transferred to boards to dry.

This kind of work is done both by men and women, but the latter are by far the best workers.

More recently hundreds of women and girls are employed in the Oji and Yokkaichi paper mills, where machinery is used for making paper from straw and wood pulp.

Toys for children, flower hairpins, ornamental combs, hair ornaments, scent-bags, and much other fine work are made by the women of Tokio, Kioto and Nagoya. The most lucrative employments for women are dressmaking (kimonos), washing and starching; and many women make good livings in these ways. In cities some childless women or widows work in dry goods shops. In the country, women generally dress their own hair, but in the cities there are professional women hairdressers who go around to different houses to dress the hair artistically, and even servants employ hairdressers.

## MINING.

In the mining districts much of the work is done by the women, especially in separating the minerals from the ores. This needs a delicacy of touch which women possess in a high degree. In the copper mines of Ashio in Shimotsuke, Kusa-kura and Omoya of Echigo, Ani of Ugo, Osaruzawa of Riku-chiu, etc., and in the silver mines of Aikawa of Sado, Handa of Iwashiro, Innai of Ugo, Osaka and Karui of Riku-chiu, etc., women are largely engaged in such work.

Girls from seven to eight years old are sent early to the working places to see the elder girls at work so that when twelve years are reached they also can earn six sen each day.

The wages received varies according to the age and skill of each worker.

At the Sado gold mines a good workwoman can earn more than twenty-five sen a day. It is wonderful to see how rapidly they distinguish one mineral from another, the sense of touch in the tips of the fingers being their only guide.

Once an experiment was made to see if there would be more profit if a machine was used for this work, so one was purchased from some foreigners and a trial was made. The machine was expected to do the work of several hundred women's days work in less than four hours; but, strange to say, it was found that the delicacy and skill of the women's fingers far surpassed the work of the machine, and the sum of the women's wages was no greater than the amount paid when the work was done by the machine. This incredible result caused them to throw aside the machine and again employ women. This proves the dexterity of women's fingers.

TRADE.

Women have never taken a very active part in trade. Firms who have several stores or wealthy merchants, do not permit women to serve in the shops, but in the smaller retail shops men go out to do the buying and let their wives and daughters do the selling: as they are more amiable and more liable to attract customers.

Although women do not engage much in active business, the name of *"Hisagi"* (the saleswoman) has been known from the most ancient times.

In the year of Taiho, A. D. 702, a public notice was given in regard to trade. It said, "Men and women must have seats apart from each other in those shops that sell anything on the street." This notice shows that women had taken some trade into their hands.

We often read in tales and other writings about women selling things in the street during the year of *Engi*. In *Utsubo-Monogatari* (one of the most ancient tales), it says, "The women who keep shops on the street, buy from the carts fish and salt, and arrange them for sale." Again, from the time of the *Fujiwara* family to the latter part of the *Kamakura* Shoguns, women must have been engaged in buying and selling. In the roll of painting called *"Nenjugiogi* Emaki" (which shows all the occurrences of the period), painted by *Mitsunaga, Gashi Zasshi* of *Nobuzane Kasuya Gongen Kenki* and *Ishiyama Engi*, and others; we can see in many of the sketches women engaged in trade, selling dry goods and various things; also some carrying eatables on their heads and selling them.

From the last part of the power of the *Kamakura* Shoguns to the reign of the *Ashikaga* family the whole country was like a great battlefield, and all communication between the cities and provinces was entirely cut off. The consequence was trade suffered exceedingly.

During this warlike period every class, the *samurai* (military class), the farmers, and even the lower classes, were obliged to fight or do some kind of warlike service away from home.

The women, while they cared for their homes during the absence of their husbands, must necessarily have cultivated the fields, spun and wove, and traded in order to make a living. This must have induced women to engage in trade, and they have continued it until this day.

In the "roll of 71 workmen" (mentioned before), many trades are represented by women, such as sellers of rice, peas, linen, cotton, lacquer, fans, obi (sashes), powder, rouge, etc. Also fish women, basket carriers, and many other small trades are represented in these pictures.

When the *Tokugawa* Shogun built a castle at Yedo (Tokyo), in the period of *Genwa*, the whole country was in a state of quietness and peace. Population increased year by year, and agriculture and commerce became prosperous; but along with this came idleness and luxury for the higher classes.

The women of the capital spent their time in amusing them
selves in music and dancing. They neglected their duties and
did not exert themselves as they did in the time of war.

After the Revolution of Meiji, 1868, many Samurai
families went into trade, and the women were often much
occupied in helping their husbands.

Now, we see shops of toilet articles, earthenwares, dried
fish, vegetables, clothes, clogs, umbrellas, tobacco, cakes and
different kinds of sweets, thread, toys, etc., kept by women,
who are very energetic and clever at the business.

In some country places tea houses and other little shops
are kept entirely by women, who at the same time spin and
care for the house during the absence of their husbands, who
are busy in cultivating the land and other work. In the
bazaars of the different cities women wait upon the customers,
and generally the hotels, restaurants, boat houses and tea
houses have female servants, and the owner of many of the
above is often a woman.

Besides these there are traveling saleswomen in different
districts.

In Osaka are *kombu* (seaweed) sellers. This seaweed
is brought from Hokkaido and prepared for sale in Osaka.
Women in parties of five to ten travel around the country
selling this seaweed and share the losses or gains. Sometimes one woman hires several others and goes round with
them superintending the selling. Another kind of seaweed
called "*Nori*" is sold in the same manner.

If we were to speak more in detail of the productive
occupations of women our readers would become weary;
enough has been said to fully show that more than one-half
of the labor in our "country" is done by the women.

# CHAPTER VII.

## ACCOMPLISHMENTS OF JAPANESE WOMEN.

These may be classified under the general heads of Poetry, Painting, Tea Ceremonies, Incense Burning, Floral Arrangements and Music. In the old methods of education these six accomplishments were taught to all girls more or less as a means of improving their morals and manners.

It is thought that the mind is enlarged by the study of poetry and painting, as "Learning the new by searching the old" is a well known proverb.

In the practice of the tea ceremony good manners and politeness are supposed to be inculcated. In floral arrangements and incense burning girls are taught to understand the value of tranquility and calmness. In this manner the ideas of women are brought to a higher condition and they become more anxious to improve.

As music is the most refined of all accomplishments it will be described in detail, together with the various instruments in use, both in the past and present periods of time.

### Music.

There are four kinds of music in use at present in Japan, viz.: Classical, European, Chinese and popular music.

#### I. CLASSICAL MUSIC.

By clasical music we mean the original Japanese music and the Chinese and Corean which were introduced about one thousand years ago. Not much later a school of music was established at the Court and all Court musicians were obliged to learn both the original and the imported music. The different styles have been handed down to the present generation of Court musicians. Although these peculiar styles of imported music have entirely passed away in their native countries they are still in use in Japan.

In the original Japanese music great use was made of metrical verses or words, while in the Chinese and Corean music dancing took the principal place rather than words. The instruments are of great variety. Classical music is considered very elegant but is rarely learned by women.

## II. EUROPEAN MUSIC.

European music was brought into this country in 1879 or '80. The instruments now in use are the organ, piano, violin, cornet and violoncello. Some music is sung with Japanese words united to the foreign notes, and some musical pieces are composed according to the European scale and played upon the koto, samisen and other Japanese instruments. The latter method is now taught in different schools.

In this connection we must mention the name of an experienced American music teacher, Mr. L. W. Mason, who was employed by the Department of Education to teach music in the new academy of music established in 1880. He adapted old Japanese airs to the foreign scale and accomplished a great deal for the development of school music.

The methods of teaching are similar to those of the West, so a description of that detail is quite unnecessary.

## III. CHINESE MUSIC.

This music has lately been introduced into this country and is sung in the Chinese language, accompanied by Gekkin, Kokiu, Teikin (all stringed instruments), and is very popular among ladies.

The Chinese scale with the different pronunciations is appended:

Jan,   cha,   kon,   han,   rin,   sin,   i,   jan.
          tee                          ha
do     re     mi     fa     sol    la     si     do.

There are two styles of Chinese music. Nagasaki and Keian styles. Although they differ in regard to time and movement they are one in origin.

Popular music is in contrast to classical music, and is very generally understood. This includes many different styles, but those that are mostly studied by girls are *Koto* music, *Naganta* (long verse): *Kouta* (short verse or folk song) and *Joruri* (a kind of operatic music).

As to the subjects of the composition, they differ very much. Some are interesting old narratives set to music, while others are descriptions of the four seasons. Some are congratulations on the long continued reign of the sovereign or on the prosperity of relatives and friends. Others are addressed to a hero protecting the orphan of his Lord against an enemy and thereby risking his own 'life; or to a delicate woman, who, although pursued by poverty and suffering ever preserves her virtue; or to some intrepid hero (chevalier), who, while protecting the weak, or chastening the strong, at last sacrifices his own life.

Such tales as these are sung accompanied by various instruments and make a deep impression upon the minds of the listeners.

Again, some are love stories which show the fulfillment of virtue when prompted by affection: there are often short verses composed impromptu about ordinary things seen or heard, and which deeply affect the mind.

As a matter of course, when the meaning differs, the music must necessarily change. Again, when the styles differ, the same music is played somewhat differently.

A short account of the different instruments used in playing popular music, the use of the scales, harmony, and the different methods of teaching may not be uninteresting.

### DIFFFRENT MUSICAL INSTRUMENTS.

The instruments used in popular music are of three kinds: Stringed instruments, such as the *koto, samisen* and *kokiu;* reed instruments, such as the *flute* and *shaku hachi;* and leather instruments, as the drum, *tsuzumi,* both large and small.

The *koto* is made of the wood of the paullownia-imperialis; it is hollow inside and has thirteen strings spread over its whole length of about six feet four inches, the breadth at the head is about nine inches, narrowing a little towards the foot. Each string is supported by a movable bridge by which the instrument is turned and it is played with the fingers shielded by ivory half-thimbles on the thumb, first and second fingers of the right hand.

If the *koto* is accompanied by the *samisen* and *kokiu* it is often called "the musical trio," and if the *shakuhachi* is added it produces very good harmony, and is very enjoyable in the open air, under the trees, amid blossoms, or in the beautiful moonlight.

The *koto* first came from China and was called *So*, and was generally learned by ladies of high rank.

There are several varieties of the "*Koto*" as "*ichigenkin*" (one stringed koto), "*Nigenkin*" and "*Yakumogoto*" (both two stringed kotos). The first two are sometimes accompanied by the *samisen*. As the latter is our original instrument, and is played only to glorify the gods, so the words or verses are very much like a hymn and are considered a sacred music. Therefore it is incumbent upon performers to cleanse their mouths and wash their hands before beginning to play.

The "*Samisen*" consists of three parts, the head, the neck and the body. The length is about three feet and it is made of a hard wood called *kwarin* (quince) or *shitan*. The body has a prepared cat's skin stretched over it on both sides. The three strings are attached to the instrument from the bottom of the body to the head by means of pegs.

The form of the *samisen* and the manner of playing it is somewhat like the guitar; the differences are that the shape of the *samisen* is nearly square, while that of the guitar is nearly round, and while the latter is played with the fingers the former is played upon with a "*bachi*" (a peculiar kind of broad stick).

The strings of the *samisen* are made of silk, decreasing in size from the 1st to the 3d. The *samisen* is the instrument most generally in use. "*Nagauta*," "*Kouta*" and "*Joruri*" (three different styles of singing) are always accompanied by it. When played with the *koto* it is the auxiliary instrument; the *kokiu* and the *shakahachi* are also auxiliary instruments to either the *koto* or the *samisen;* and also the flute, drums and the large and small *tsuzumi*. For singing *joruri* no other instrument is used except the *samisen*. The history of the *samisen* is very uncertain. Some say that it came originally from the Loo-choo islands in the period of *Enroku*, and was then called *jabisen* (covered with a snakeskin called ja). A blind musician named Nakanokoji used it at first. It had then but two strings, he added another string, and instead of the cover of snakeskin he used a prepared cat's skin, consequently the name *ja-bi-sen* was changed to *samisen*. This account is, however, denied by some writers, as in old books written before that period the word *samisen* is mentioned.

There is reason to believe that the *samisen* did not come from either Korea or the Loo-choo Islands. The probability is that it was brought here by the Portuguese from some more southern country. Such musical instruments are now seen in India and in the neighboring countries.

The Kokiu is also said to have come from the Loo-choo Islands, as well as the *samisen*. It was originally called "*Rabeca*," which is a Portuguese word, and is the same as "Rebec" in English.

This was no doubt a Moorish musical instrument, and made its way into Spain and Portugal and thence into the different countries of Europe, and thus through the Portuguese found its way into Japan, about three hundred years ago. Originally it had but two strings, but string after string was added, until out of it was evolved the present violin; thus the kokiu and the violin may have had the same origin. The *samisen* and the *kokiu* are the same in form, only the kokiu is a little smaller.

The *samisen* is played with a "*bachi*," while the *kokiu* is played with a bow, and we do not know how long since this difference existed.

The *kokiu* and the violin are both played with bows, only the former is not held under the chin, but is held vertically upon the lap by the left hand.

The *shaku hachi* and the flute are both made of bamboo. The former is played like a cornet. Both are played by men and very seldom by women.

### THE DRUM AND THE LARGE AND SMALL TSUZUMI.

The drum is placed upon a kind of frame or stand and is beaten with two drum-sticks. The large *tsuzumi* is placed upon the left knee and the small *tsuzumi* upon the right shoulder. Both are supported by the left hand and are beaten by the right hand put closely together.

If both large and small *tsuzumi* are played by a single person at the same time the positions of the instruments are not changed, only the large *tsuzumi* is held by the left elbow being placed upon the left knee, while the small *tsuzumi* is placed upon the right shoulder held by the left hand. Then both are alternately beaten by the right fingers, the hand being carried up and down very rapidly.

The small *tsuzumi* has a silk cord attached to the instrument. The sound may be changed to a greater or less volume by tightening or loosening this cord with the left hand while holding the instrument upon the right shoulder.

As in other countries, drums are only used as auxiliary instruments for giving tune and activity to other music. In *nagauta* and *kouta* they are used as auxiliaries, but never as chief instruments.

### THE SCALES OF POPULAR MUSIC.

The scales of popular music follow those of classical music and are of twelve semi-tones (chromatic action-scale). But in popular music the minor scale is generally used.

There are three ways of tuning the *samisen* in general use: They are "*Honchoshi*" (standard), "*Niagari*" (2d string higher), and "*Sansagari*" (3d string lower).

The following are the three ways of tuning:

#### "HONCHOSHI."

| do | fa | do |
|----|----|----|
| 1st string. | 2d string. | 3d string. |

"*Niagari*" (2d string higher).

| do | sol | do |
|----|-----|----|
| 1st string. | 2d string. | 3d string. |

"*Sansagari*" (3d string lower).

| do | fa | si |
|----|----|----|
| 1st string. | 2d string. | 3d string. |

Alterations or variations of the melody may occur in the midst of a composition, from "*Honchoshi*" to either "*Niagari*" or "*Sansagari*" or *vice versa*.

When more than two *samisens* are played together, one or two may play different notes, putting in some additional notes now and then, thus making the music more harmonious and interesting. This is called "*Uwajoshi*," while the ordinary mode of playing is called "*Honjamisen*."

To play "*Uwajoshi*," a piece of wood, ivory or tortoise-shell about one inch long called "*Kase*," is tied by a string to the neck of the *samisen*, five or six inches below the head (somewhat like a "dumb" on a violin, but this serves to make the note higher).

If "*honjamisen*" be of "*honchoshi*" the "*uwajoshi*" must be tuned "*niagari*," if the former be "*niagari*" the latter must be "*sansagari;*" the first string of the "*uwajoshi*" must always be tuned to the same tone as the second of the "*honjamisen*." The different ways of tuning the *koto* are "*Kumoi*," "*Hira-joshi*" and a few others. The theory of music was formerly not studied as much as practical performance upon various instruments. (See pages 124, 125, 126.)

### THE METHODS OF TEACHING POPULAR MUSIC, REVIEWS AND CONCERTS.

Girls usually begin to study popular music from the age of 6 and 7. Although from quite early times a certain kind of notation existed, it is not in general use. Therefore pupils have nothing to rely upon but their memories and the constant practice of the ear and the hand. An example of the methods of teaching by a "*Nagauta*" teacher will illustrate.

A simple melody is selected and the beginner is made to sing with the teacher until the words are well learned. Then the teacher hands a *samisen* to the pupil. Now the *samisen* has no note board as on a guitar or on a Chinese Gekkin, so there is no indication of the manner of playing upon the instrument: the teacher therefore holds the fingers of the pupil and carries them up and down on the neck of the *samisen* till the melody is well learned. Then the teacher sitting opposite to the pupil plays and sings the whole over and over until perfectly satisfied with the result. What an amount of patience must be possessed both by the teacher and pupil! Without great effort for several years no skill can be acquired.

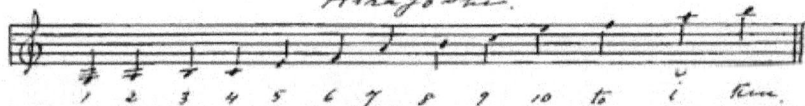
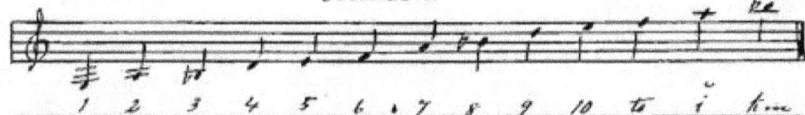
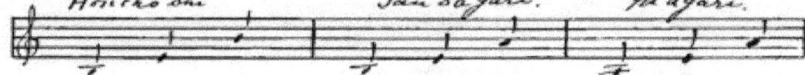

# Rokudan

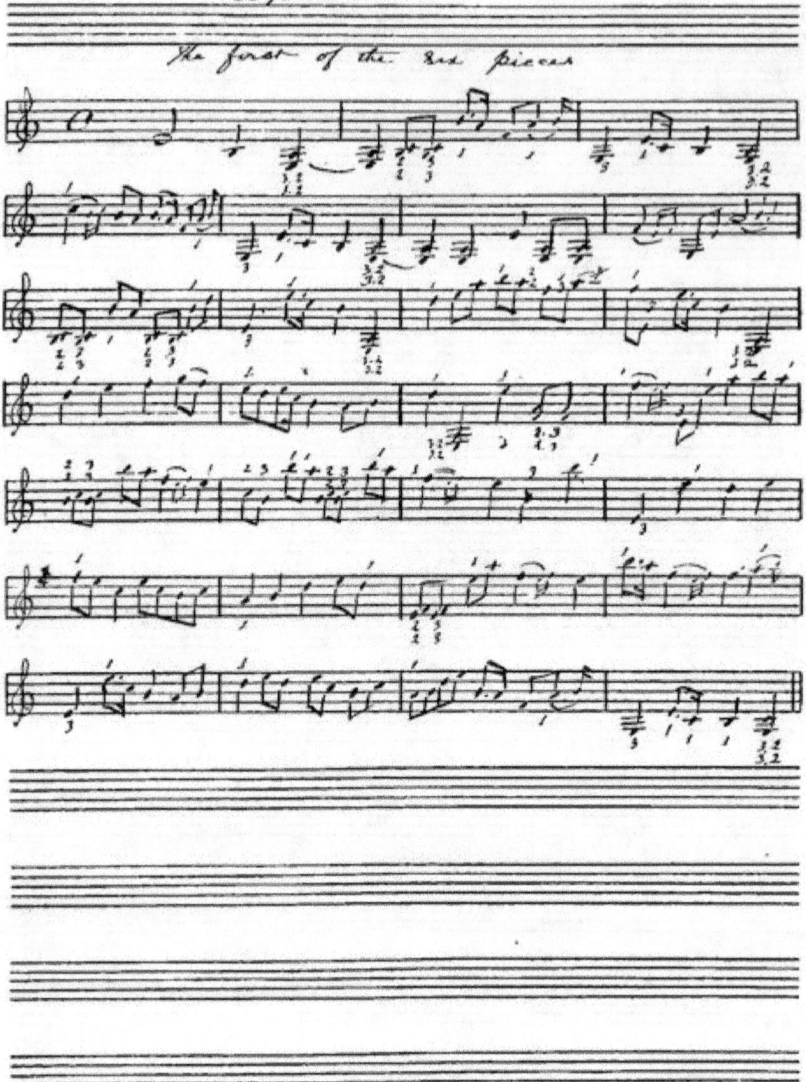
The first of the six pieces

The Spring Flowers (3rd verse)

With *koto* music almost the same process is necessary; but on this instrument, as each string has a settled tone, if it be once tuned, it is not so difficult to learn as the *samisen*.

The music teachers hold reviews or concerts once or twice each season. This is to give pupils an opportunity to exhibit their skill. Other teachers and pupils are invited and by hearing solos played and choruses sung much emulation is excited and all present are improved by the exercise of their talents.

### THE CHANGES AND PROGRESS OF MUSIC, DANCING AND THE DRAMA.

This is the present condition of popular music. As for its changes and progress from early times we cannot minutely describe them in this brief account. Singing and dancing have been practiced in Japan from very early times, but after an importation from China and Corea, our original styles were forgotten. Imported music is not only preserved in its original form, but has also been changed in many ways. Some melodies have been composed according to the taste of our people, making use of foreign instruments. In the book of laws called "*Taihorei*," finished in the eighth century, we find the following: "*Gagakurio*, the 'Institute of Music,' was established at the court, and the music of China, Koma, Kudara, Shiragi and Kure were taught."

"Our original music consisted of songs and dances. Therefore thirty men singers, 100 women singers and 100 dancers were placed in the Institute."

The only instrument used for Japanese music was the flute, but in Chinese music there were several instruments, as the *sho* (flute), *kuko* (kind of harp), *so* (koto), *biwa, hokei*, (stone gongs), drums, *shaku-hachi, hichiriki* (a kind of hautboy), etc.

The music taught in this Institute was mostly used on great ceremonial occasions at the Court and is generally called "*Ga ga-ku*" (classical music), and many of those melodies have come down to the present day. Among the Chinese instruments in general use were the flute, *sha ku-hachi*, So or *koto, biwa*, etc. The two latter were chiefly played by the ladies. As this music came into general use new tunes with verses were composed. The "*Saibara*" and "*Kagura*" dances may be dated from the ninth century. Besides these dances, which belonged to classical music, there were other kinds of dances and sports, such as "*Sangaku*" and "*Dengaku*." The former, also called "*Sarugaku*," was a funny kind of play, and was the beginning of the comic drama (ninth century). In the last part of the fourteenth century this was changed to a peculiar kind of song and musical performance of *Kanze* and *Komparu* styles (the No dance of the present time). "*Dengaku*," originally a kind of rustic music, was mixed with comedies of *Sangaku* (twelfth century) and became very popular, and the professionals called "*Dengaku-hoshi*" began to appear.

Although women did not take part in comic performances they used to dance in men's clothes and were called "*Shira-bioshi*" or *Otoko-mai*, which became very popular about the twelfth century.

In the last part of the tenth century there were blind men who told historical narratives, accompanied by the *Biwa*.

After the war between the *Genji* and the *Heike* families these blind musicians used to tell of the events that took place during the battles. So eagerly were these stories received that the name of "*Heike*" was given to the performance.

In the first part of the twelfth century new religious sects sprung up. By prayers, accompanied with singing and dancing, and sometimes with a certain kind of theatrical performance, these sects tried to attract the attention of the people and make them interested in religion. There were also priests who preached sermons and sung narratives in songs to interest their audiences. From this a peculiar kind of sermon originated. Later this was changed to the odes, lectures, war stories, witticisms, etc., of the present day. From these sermons and the "*Heike*" sprung up the *Joruri* (sixteenth century). It is commonly believed that *Ono-no Otsu* (an attendant of the famous *Hideyoshi*) was the originator of the story, but there is evidence that it was known before her time.

"*Joruri*" was the name of a lady in the story, and as the incidents recited or sung were greatly appreciated by the people, her name was given to the music just as the name "*Heike*" was given to a somewhat similar performance.

Since then "*Joruri*" has been greatly improved by being sung with the *samisen*, and new tunes with different ideas have been composed. Great composers began to appear and many different styles were formed, such as *Gidaiu, Itchiu, Kato, Shinnai, Kiyomoto, Tokiwazu,* etc. There are many women who make their living by playing "*Joruri*."

In the last part of the sixteenth century theatrical performances were undertaken by women, and as a woman named *Okuni* was the originator it was called "*Okuni Theatre.*" A change was made here from the dancing prayers and other musical plays. (*No-kiogen.*) The women's theatre, however, was prohibited in the seventeenth century and young men took their place, and this custom continues to the present day. The story of "*Joruri*" was at first represented by using dolls (as marionettes), but from the year 1700 the actors performed themselves. Although the prohibition was taken off from actresses they were not allowed to play on the same stage as the men, so young actors have to take the parts of women, and do so with great skill. Although women do not perform on the public stage, yet there are many lady dancing teachers and dancing girls who entertain people at parties and dance and sing before large numbers.

### THE PRESENT CONDITION OF DANCING.

As dancing accompanied by *koto* music represents the meaning of the songs, so some dances are of elegant character, and are called "*Mai;*" while others are of a lower order and are called "*Odori,*" of which there are two kinds; one consists of movements of the hands and feet, somewhat like European pantomime. In the other kind words are spoken, accompanied by movements. Each movement represents the meaning of the words, and the spectators are moved by feelings of sadness, anger and mirth. If well danced, hand-clapping or other signs of applause indicate the pleasure of the audience. Girls learn the "*odori*" dances from six to about nineteen, and no girl over that age dances unless she is a teacher. Until about twenty years ago physical training was much neglected, gymnastic exercises for girls were unknown, and ladies were mostly engaged in sedentary occupations. Now many parents have their daughters taught "*odori*" to develop their physical strength, besides it is thought that girls who have practiced dancing acquire more grace in their movements. These are some of the reasons why so many girls are now learning "*odori*."

When girls dance the "*odori*" on ordinary occasions they do so in their usual dresses, but when they have a dancing performance it is upon a stage with a curtain and other theatrical accessories, such as artificial hair and costumes to represent certain characters. Recently European dancing has become quite fashionable among the higher classes.

In some parts of the country there are women who dance sacred dances in the temples. There is still another kind of dancing very popular in country places, somewhat like that of *Dengaku*. This is danced from the 13th to the 16th of July. Young men and women go out to the fields in the evening. Here they form a large circle, a leader who is a good singer is selected among them, who sings the first verse, all the others joining in the chorus, clapping their hands or moving them to the right or left, or marching up and down following the singer, thus reminding one a little of a quadrille or a country dance.

## The Tea Ceremony.

The tea ceremony, usually called *Cha-no-yu* is the art of making tea and serving it to invited guests. Sometimes dinner and *sake* are also served. The ceremony of offering these viands is attended with great solemnity, as there are certain rules for every movement of the hands and feet which must be strictly observed. But even this solemnity indicates great respect, and host, as well as guests, must pay strict attention to every little point of etiquette. The principal virtue to be observed is kindness, as anyone who is carefully taught in the tea ceremony is trained to gentleness and will naturally learn to be cautious. This is one of the reasons why women were required to learn this accomplishment.

*Cha-no-yu* had its origin at the time of the *Ashikaga* government and it has flourished ever since the time of the *Shogun Yoshimasa*. The special rules or ceremonies were not settled until the time of *Toyotomi Hideyoshi* ("*Taiko*"). An attendant of the "*Taiko*" named *Sen-no-Rikin*, who was also a professor of the tea ceremony, compiled many rules and they have been handed down to the present day.

The tea ceremony has passed through some changes, so that many styles have been fashionable from time to time. The style which originated with *Rikiu* was called *Senke* style, from this came both *Omote Senke* and *Ura Senke*. Oribe, Yabu-uchi, Enshiu and Sekishu styles are the subdivisions of these with more or less changes in each, but in all are the same principles.

*Usu-cha* (weak tea) and *Koi-cha* (strong tea). *Koi-cha* is obtained from the buds of the tea plant picked at the time of the first crop; the *Usu-cha* is the buds of the second crop. Both have to go through a certain process to be made fit to drink, and must also be reduced to a powder in tea grinders or tea mills.

The best tea is obtained from the village of *Uji* in *Yamashiro*.

The ceremony for both *Koi-cha* and *Usu-cha* differs in some points. The marked difference is that it is more complicated in *Koi-cha* than in the *Usu-cha*. In *Koi-cha* only one cup of tea is served by the host to a number of guests and each one after sipping a few mouthfuls passes the cup to his neighbor and so on; in *Usu-cha* the host serves to each guest a cup in turn.

THE CHA-NOYU OR TEA ROOM.

The tea room is built very small (generally of four and a half mats), the ceiling is low, the entrance narrow and low and all the finish must be simple, although elegant in style. The ornaments consist of a hanging picture (*kakemono*), an incense burner, flower vase, and there may be one or two small bronzes. A fire place called a *ro* is cut in the floor about fourteen inches square, it is made of stone, and a fire-dog called *gotoku* is placed in the ashes, upon which a kettle is put.

In building a tea room great care is taken in regard to the choice of timber for the pillars or supporters of the *tokonoma* (recess). For these the wood is sometimes left with the bark on and sometimes highly polished after the bark has been removed. Neither paint nor other ornamentation is used. If possible, timber of some rare wood is used and a large sum of money is frequently paid for only a single pillar. The garden attached to the tea room must be arranged by the hands of a skillful gardener who makes a specialty of this kind of garden.

The tea utensils are of many kinds. By a very slight difference of shape different names are given to the same things. This is owing to the desire for old-fashioned things. For example, calling a certain kind of tea ladle "*Sojun's* tea ladle," or a spoon "*Rikiu's* spoon," etc. But it must be understood that competition in luxury was not the true object of the tea ceremony. The following are the necessary articles used in or for "*Cha-no-yu:*"

1. A portable furnace made of pottery, brass or of iron, is used from the 1st of May to the end of October. At other times the *ro* is opened.

2. Kettles or pots for boiling water, are of many varieties, but all are of iron, often highly ornamented.

3. Charcoal holder or scuttle, made of bamboo, or a box made of wisteria vine, or any kind of wood that one prefers.

4. *Gotoku*, a three-legged iron stand to support the kettle over the fire. The one used in the portable furnace differs from that used in *ro*.

5. Kettle mats; paper is properly used, but sometimes mats made of split rattan or interlaced wood are used.

6. Feather brush.

7. Water jar, either of porcelain or of copper.

8. Incense burner, of porcelain, wood without paint, lacquer or of copper.

9. Cup, of many varieties.

10. Napkin or tea towel, of silk, usually of purple, red or of tea color.

11. Teaspoon, of bamboo, ivory or of lacquer work.

12. *Koboshi*, a vessel to pour the hot water into, made of porcelain, copper or of wood.

13. Flower vase; the vase to be set on the floor and the one to be hung up on a nail are of porcelain or of copper; the vase when hung by a string from the ceiling is of copper.

14. Tea jar, of lacquer or of earthenware of either Japanese or of Chinese workmanship. These jars have different

names according to the shape and material. For instance, *"natsume"* is of lacquer, the shape resembling *natsume* (dates). There are others called *kawataro, goke fubuki, nakatsugi,* etc.

15. Coverings or bags for the tea sets of silk brocade, satin and other old fabrics.

16. Cover supporter, of a bamboo ring or earthenware, also of copper made in shapes of dolls or crabs, etc.

17. A tea stirrer made of bamboo, split at one end and made to stir the powdered tea in the hot water.

18. *Daisu,* cabinet, generally of fine old lacquer or shelves for packing away the tea sets.

### THE RULES OF CHA-NO-YU.

The rules of Cha-no-yu are not alike in different styles. When the portable furnace is used the ceremony differs from that when *ro* is used, also that of *koi-cha* is different from *usu-cha.* The whole ceremony is too complicated to attempt describing it in full, but the *koi-cha-kwai* at which sake and dinner are served may be briefly sketched.

### KOI-CHA PARTY.

When one is to give a *koi-cha-kwai* or party, the host sends out the invitations with the names of all the invited guests, the name of the principal guest being written at the head of the list. This is sent out by a messenger who goes from house to house. The invited guests then meet at the house of the principal guest (in all about five) and talk about the dresses they ought to wear at the party, or consult about the place to wait. Then each guest goes to the host and expresses thanks for the kind invitation. This is called "the previous call for thanks."

On the appointed day all the guests go promptly to the house and wait, sitting on benches at the waiting place. When all have arrived they give a signal to the host. He hearing it, after having swept the tea house, comes out and greets the guests, the latter saluting him and each other wash their hands and clean their mouths, then slip into the tea room through the narrow entrance, look at the hanging picture and the kettle on the *ro,* or on the portable furnace with critical admiration, and then arrange themselves on the mats.

The host, waiting till all the guests are seated, enters, makes another salutation, looks at the charcoal to see if it is all right, again makes a bow, and telling them that the dinner will soon be served retires, closing the entrance door to the kitchen. After a few minutes the host brings in the "*dai*" or small low tables for each guest, with several dishes upon them, and asking them to begin to eat, again goes out.

The guests, bowing to each other, begin to eat. The host makes his appearance again, and requesting them to eat and drink freely, again disappears. Leaving them alone for some time he returns and drinks sake with each guest.

It is the rule that everything that is offered should be eaten, but in case one cannot possibly eat all the remnants must be taken home in a bag brought for the purpose. The host on his part takes care to provide such dishes and in such portions that the guests may eat all that is placed before them.

The manner of taking the food from the host, or placing it on the floor, etc., must be according to the established rules of etiquette. When the dinner is over the host brings on some sweets for each person to take home, and telling them to take a short recess again disappears. As for the guests they put the sweets in their pockets and retire to the waiting place.

The host, finding the room vacated, sweeps it, changes the ornaments, and invites the guests once more to the same room by striking upon a musical gong. After they are all seated the host again opens the kitchen entrance and making a bow brings in fire-sticks, feather brush, etc., feeds the charcoal and prepares for making tea. Meanwhile the guests praise the beauty of the fireplace, ashes and the manner of putting on the charcoal.

The host then places all the necessary tea sets in front of him, folds up the bags, creases the napkin through his hand in a peculiar manner and wipes the cups, puts a few spoonfuls of powdered tea in it, pours on a dipper half full of hot water, twice stirs it with a bamboo stirrer, which is then laid on the mats; the host then places himself opposite the principal guest. The latter then moves forward one step on his knee to receive the cup from the host, returns to his seat, and bowing to his neighbors drinks one sip and praises the excellent taste of the tea. At this moment the host returns to his former seat.

Each guest drinks three sips and passes the cup to the next person and so on. The last one finishing the tea brings the cup back to the principal guest, who returns it to the host with low bows. After a few moments the guests all bow together.

The host promises the guests to make usu-cha for them a little later. The guests acknowledge their pleasure by bows. The host then begins to put away the tea utensils. This is the time for the guests to express a desire to examine the teaspoon, the tea jar and bags. The host first takes the *"natsume"* (tea-jar) in his right hand, puts it on the left palm with the right hand, creases the napkin and wipes it and places them all in a row before the guests.

Then the guests take them up, one by one, and make inquiries as to the age and the places from whence they came, and admire and praise them. Besides these they have many other things to see and admire, but this must all be done according to established rules. Great care is taken in handling these things on both sides. This is to show respect to each other and to endeavor not to make any mistakes in etiquette. The *Cha-no-yu* ceremony is short, symbolizes tranquility, politeness and conscientiousness.

When *koi-cha* is over, the host serves *usu-cha* for each guest. Both parties now lay aside all ceremonies and rules and are allowed to speak familiarly with each other. In *koi-cho-kwai* the host has to do everything without the help of servants or waiters, although he may be a very rich and noble person. The guests therefore know that the host may be very tired, and as soon as the ceremony is over it is well for them to leave. On the day following the guests have to call upon the host and express their thanks for the kind treatment of the previous day. We have thus gone through the whole ceremony of the *koi-cha kwai*.

### GAMES.

There are several games that go with the tea ceremony, such as several persons arranging some flowers in a vase in turn according to their own taste, they then compare, criticise or praise.   This is called " *Mawaribana.*"

*Chakabuki* is another game.   The host makes several cups of different kinds of tea, and the guests have to guess the names.   This is somewhat similar to that of incense guessing. These and many other game are played by ladies at the tea parties.

## Burning Incense.

The object of burning incense is to criticise the odor of different incenses, and to guess their names by inhaling their odors.   So it partakes more of the nature of a game than a pure accomplishment, but as it was practiced anciently in our country, it must be included as one of the accomplishments of ladies.

### THE CHANGES AND PROGRESS OF INCENSE.

The perfume of good incense gives pleasure to the sense of smell, just as beautiful colors please the eye and pleasant sounds the ear.   It is therefore quite natural that we should love pleasant odors, as from the beginning of man's existence fragrant flowers or anything that has a sweet smell, has been found agreeable.

The use of perfumes as a means of pleasing the sense of smell probably begun later than the arts of music or painting. Incense burning was first practiced when Buddhism was brought into our country.   Incense is always burned when Buddha is worshiped, and at the same time different kinds of music also came from India and China.   As the people of Japan liked this incense they began to burn it to scent the dress or hair, or to fill the room with a pleasant odor.   Perfumes that come from Europe or America are generally in liquid form, but ours are solid and must be burned in order to emit any odor.

Incense is not made of one simple material, but has many ingredients, so the quality of the incense depends upon the manner of mixing these ingredients, and it is difficult to always attain success.   It is mostly made by ladies and may very properly be classed among the fine arts and compared to the harmony produced by musical sounds and by the blending of colors.

Games have been invented in which different incenses are burned so they may be compared and criticised. For instance, several persons take the same ingredients and mix them in different proportions, as they think best, thus making great varieties of incense. These are burned, one by one, by a competent judge and carefully criticised. In very ancient times this game was much enjoyed, but at present, game of smelling and thus guessing the names of the incense is the only one played. The most common of these games are *Jusshuko*, *Genji-ko*, *Ogusa-ko*, *Kodori-ko*, etc.

AN INCENSE PARTY.

This is a most refined entertainment, and suitable for ladies with which to occupy their leisure hours; there are many among the higher classes who are well acquainted with this game. It is a very expensive entertainment, and the difficulties in learning it have greatly retarded the development of the art.

When a lady is invited to an incense party she must stop smoking, drinking tea or eating sweets for at least twenty-four hours in advance of accepting the invitation. She must also be careful not to use pomatum, perfume or oil. Anything that has an odor must be avoided lest it should prevent the incense from giving out a pure scent. When a guest enters the room where the burning is going on, great care must be taken to open and shut the door quietly, and every movement must be very gentle. In case one is obliged to stand or leave the room, care must be taken not to disturb the air for fear of banishing the fragrance.

The host now burns the different kinds of incense in a burner, and places it before the guests. The latter in turn smell it, and whichever name they think is right put the name cards into a box arranged for the purpose. When all have finished the box is opened and the cards are counted The one who has the greatest number of names right wins the game, of course the others all lose. At the time of putting the cards into the box all speaking is forbidden. It is also the rule that no one must smell more than three to five times of any one kind of incense.

The most common game is *Jusshu-ko* (ten different incenses), of which we will give a short account. *Jusshu-ko* consists of four different incenses made into ten little parcels.

Three parcels of No. 1; three parcels of No. 2; three parcels of No. 3; one parcel of the incense named "guest," in all making ten parcels. An extra parcel of No. 1, No. 2 and No. 3 is burned first, and the guests smell them as samples of the others. This is called the "Trial Incense." The parcel named "guest" is not tried. Then the host puts all the parcels together and takes one of them and burns it. The guests in turn take up the incense-burner and smell it, and comparing the odor with those smelt as trial, put in the box the name card of any number they may decide upon. But if one thinks it is not the smell of any incense smelt for the trial, then the card of the "guest" may be put into the box. When all the incense has been burned, the box is opened and the following record may be found: In the record—"Young pine," "Red plum," etc., are the cards the players have received to represent their names.

The record of *Jusshu-ko*.

### THE NAMES OF INCENSE.

No. 1.  *Tamatsumi.*
No. 2.  *Shibafune.*
No. 3.  *Mumei.*
  U.  *Nobort uma* (U is the "guest.")

### INCENSE BURNED.

III. I. u. II. I. III. II. I. III. II.

| | | | | | | | | | | | |
|---|---|---|---|---|---|---|---|---|---|---|---|
| Young Pine, | - | I. | III. | I. | II. | u. | I. | II. | II. | III. | III. | 3 guessed. |
| Red Plum, | - | III. | I. | II. | II. | I. | u. | III. | II. | I. | III. | 4 guessed. |
| Chrysanthemum, | - u. | I. | II. | II. | III. | I. | III. | II. | III. | I. | | 3 guessed. |
| Narcissus, | - | I. | III. | I. | III. | II. | II. | I. | III. | u. | II. | 1 guessed. |
| Bamboo, | - | III. | I. | u. | III. | I. | II. | II. | I. | III. | II. | 8 guessed. |

Name of place.                           Date.

By this record we can see that the first incense burned was Mumei No. 3, and "Young Pine," "Chrysanthemum" and "Narcissus" got it wrong, while two others guessed it correctly. The second incense was *Tamatsumi* No. 1, "Red

Plum," "Chrysanthemum" and "Bamboo" guessed it correctly. The third incense was the guest "U," and "Bamboo" only guessed it right.

The result was that "Bamboo" was found to be the most skilled, and out of ten only two were wrong. On the other hand, "Narcissus," out of ten, guessed only one right.

The underlined numbers show the kind of incense guessed.

### ARTICLES NEEDED FOR BURNING INCENSE.

A great variety of articles are needed for burning incense, such as an incense-burner, incense-box, silver-leaf fire-sticks, incense-sticks, incense-spoon, card box, etc.

An incense-burner is made either of porcelain, or copper, or iron.

An incense-box is generally of lacquer and of various shapes. One style is a trebled or three-storied box. The upper box is for holding the incense, the middle one is to hold aloes wood or agallochum, and the lower one is to put the cinders or ashes into.

The silver leaf is a small piece of mica upon which the incense is placed, and put over the fire in a burner.

The card box is to put the name or number cards in, when the game is played.

The cards are little lacquered wooden blocks with pictures of plum, bamboo, pine, chrysanthemum, etc., on one side, and a number on the other. In each set are ten cards: three of No. 1, three of No. 2, and three of No. 3, and one of "*u*" or the "guest." In playing *jussu-ko* each person takes one set or ten cards of the same picture. The picture represents the name of the owner, and the number on the other side represents the number the player notes in the game.

### THE METHODS OF MANUFACTURING INCENSE.

Incense is made of different ingredients mixed together in various proportions, thus a variety of perfumes can be made out of the same ingredients. For example *Yamaji-no-tsuyu* (the dew on the mountain path) is composed of aloes wood four parts, clover four parts, musk 0.1, koko four parts.

*Kokon* (evening twilight) is composed of aloes wood 1.6 parts, sandal wood one part, kakko one part and koko two parts.

In making these incenses the ingredients must be powdered, mixed together, then pounded, and kneaded with white
honey.

## Floral Arrangement.

Among the many beautiful things of this world, nothing
is so enjoyable and pretty as flowers, and whoever has a
heart must find pleasure in them.   In decorating or ornament-
ing a room nothing can be more appropriate.

The chief purpose in arranging flowers is to use them for
ornaments, for this reason the accomplishment is naturally
learned by women whose duty it is to decorate the house and
make it attractive.

### DIFFERENT SYSTEMS OF FLORAL ARRANGEMENT.

As this accomplishment became more and more fashionable, many different systems sprang up among which were
those of *" Ensiu "* and *" Sekishiu."*   These systems consist of
much twisting and bending to give more grace to the leaves
and branches.   On the other hand *" Koriu "* only consists in
cutting away superabundant branches or leaves.   Each has a
beauty peculiar to itself, and although there are many styles
only differing slightly from each other, all are equally beautiful and all have the same end in view, namely, "That the
arrangement of the flowers should represent the mind of the
arranger."

The idea is, that if the mind is influenced by anger,
hatred or any other violent passion, flowers can never be suc-
cessfully or gracefully arranged, but if the mind be tranquil,
or only filled with kindness and love, then will the flowers
be satisfactorily arranged.   Another essential principle is to
improve upon nature and this can only be accomplished by
a careful study of the beauties of nature.   In all the systems
pupils are taught to always keep their minds tranquil and
happy in order to produce correct designs.

### ARTICLES NEEDED IN FLORAL ARRANGEMENTS.

Although the articles needed for arranging flowers are
not the same in different styles, yet they all consist of a little
saw, a knife, a pair of scissors and different kinds of vases or
flower pots.

For a vase, porcelain is considered the best; next copper, then iron. The latter is seldom used as it is liable to rust. Some few vases are made of bamboo or wood. Names are given to them according to their shape and position, such as the "hooked vase," the suspended vase, the single-branched vase, etc. Sometimes vases are in pairs or in double pairs. In the latter case one pair is called the "principal pair," while the other is called the "secondary pair." It is the rule to arrange tree branches in blossom in the principal pairs and flowers in the secondary pairs.

## METHODS OF ARRANGING FLOWERS.

Two blossoming tree branches are taken; the one called "*Shin*" (center or principal) is made to stand in a vertical line; the other, called "*Tome*" (support or tertiary), is made to lie almost in a horizontal line with the water. Between these two another branch is added and is called "*Nagashi*" (streamer or secondary). These three branches complete one decoration. Two more branches may, however, be added, making five branches; the one added between the center and the streamer is called the "shoulder;" the other between the support and streamer is called the "body."

The seven-branch design is made by adding two branches to the above mentioned ones, to assist the center and the streamer. This design is used for very ceremonial occasions.

The nine-branch design is made by adding two more branches to the last; one is auxiliary to the "body" and the other to the "support" and are generally placed behind them.

The peculiarity of this art is the changes and variations that can be made in this nine-branch design as a foundation by adding as many as fifteen or more branches, or by lessening them.

By this arrangement the different aspects of the four seasons, the wonders of natural phenomena, the appearance of youth, age, prosperity or adversity are represented. Indeed there is no limit to the alterations and interest it affords. The appearance of flowers differ according to the seasons. Spring flowers represent new life and development, therefore they should be arranged when in full bloom. Summer flowers represent a more flourishing condition and should be arranged in great abundance. The flowers of autumn indicate a less vigorous growth and should be arranged with less profusion. Winter flowers indicate a period of rest, or the death of the year, and should be arranged with very few blossoms. The size and the number of flowers to be arranged depend upon the shape and size of the vase. If the opening of the vase be one foot square the height of the flowers, as a rule, should be one foot and a half high, that is, one whole length and a half of the vase. Some variations, however, may be allowed.

Trying to make flowers look more beautiful by putting too many branches into a little vase reminds one of a peacock spreading his tail feathers in pride, and is a vain and ludicrous attempt.

The following faults are to be avoided: a branch projecting from out or under an auxiliary branch; branches crossing each other; branches in parallel lines, or having the same height, as if they were vieing with each other; openings seen among the branches, etc.

The best time to cut flowers is early in the morning, while the dew is still upon them, and half-opened ones should be chosen, if not, the color and the fragrance will the sooner fade. In a style called " *Nagekomi*," that is, putting branches in a vase in the simplest manner, it is bad taste to put in too many, especially so if the mouth of the vase be small. It appears more tasteful to select slender branches. The vase should be filled with pure rain water, if obtainable, the next best is spring water, and after that well water.

The following are the principal flowers used in floral arrangements:

### SPRING FLOWERS.

| | |
|---|---|
| Plum blossoms. | Azaleas. |
| Cherry blossoms. | Peonies. |
| Sumomo (a kind of plum). | Forsythia suspensa. |
| Peach branches. | Fuku-ju-so. |
| Pear blossoms. | Hamanasu (a kind of rose). |
| Almond branches. | Garden marigold. |
| Willow. | Poppy. |
| Wisteria. | Calenthe discolor—Lindl. |
| Chinese flowering apple. | Orithia edulis—Mig. |
| Roses. | Sanzashi (a kind of hawthorn). |
| Corchorus. | |

## SUMMER FLOWERS.

Tachibana (a kind of citrus).
Common Indian shot.
Lotus.
Iris.
Pink.
Shakuyaku (a kind of peony).
Cape jessamine.
Day lily.
Summer chrysanthemum.
Pomegranates.
Lillies.
Great flowering clematis.

Satsuki (a kind of azalea).
Shakunagi (a kind of rose bay).
Kakitsubata (a kind of iris).
Hydrangia.
Crape-myrtle from India.
Garden balsam from India.
Morning glory.
Podocarpus Nageia-R-Br.
Blackberry lily from India.
Shaga (a kind of Iris).
Deutzia Sieboldiana, Maxim.

### AUTUMN FLOWERS.

Orchis.
Chrysanthemum.
Hagi (a kind of bush clover).
Eularia japonica, trin.
Authistiria argusus.
Shion (a kind of aster).
Platycodon grandiflorum—D. C. (a kind of gentian.)

Mokusai, oleafragrans thrmb.
Fuyoo, a kind of rose-mallow.
Omi-naeshi.
Oshiroi (a kind of four-o'clock).
Shin kaido (a kind of elephant's ear).
Kwan on so, etc., etc.

### WINTER FLOWERS.

Willows.
Camellia.
Winter chrysanthemum.
Yatsude.
Narcissus.

Robai (Japanese Allspice).
Winter peony.
Sazankwa (a kind of Japanese camellia).

Although thus classified, there are some plants that can be used through all the seasons, as the pine, bamboo and other kinds of evergreen shrubs and trees. Though they bear no flowers, their freshness, strength and their peculiar beauty which surpasses even the flowers, cause them to be used all the year round.

### A FLORAL PARTY.

A floral party is given by teachers to enable their pupils to arrange the flowers they have already studied and to permit the teachers to criticise them. These are also exhibited to the public and is a means of encouragement to greater skill.

### Painting.

Japanese painting having been much noticed by other nations, many books have been written describing its changes, progress and its different styles; therefore we will only mention that from ancient times painting was regarded as one of the most suitable accomplishments for women of the higher class. Indeed it stands first among the fine arts, and its use and application are very extensive. Very few women have, however, devoted themselves to this art as a profession; most of them have only taken their leisure time to paint, and that only for amusement. Thus we seldom find any who rivaled the professional artists. There were, however, some among the gentler sex who excelled in this art. During the ninth century names of court ladies who were famous for painting were often heard. Empresses and Princesses were also known to have painted very exquisitely. The Empresses *Somedono-no-Kisaki Kwanshi-Goreizen*, and *Takeko*, daughter of *Ono-no-Miya Sanesuke-ko;* the wives of the Lords *Nagaiye-kio, Iyenaga-kio; Eshikibu*, etc., were the most noted for their paintings, from the ninth to the eleventh century.

In the "*Genji-mono gatari*," a novel or narrative of the court, completed in the beginning of the eleventh century, also in other writings that describe the condition of those days, we read that this art was one of the accomplishments of the ladies.

The following is a short extract from the history of the "Genji" and "Heike" families called "*Genpei sei suiki*," in which mention is made of *Kiyomori's* daughters who excelled in this art. It will give a good idea of the condition of ladies and what they learned in those days:

"*Kiyomori* had eight daughters; one was married to *Kanemasa-ko*, an Imperial court officer. She was not only beautiful and benevolent, but was an unrivaled artist. She was commanded to paint on the sliding paper doors of the Imperial palace an illustration of the narrative called '*Isemo-nogatarii*' (a phœnix in a bamboo forest), and it was said to have been exquisitely done.

144

"The second daughter became the Empress. The third was married to the Governor Motozane-ko. She was noted for her great skill in playing upon the *Biwa*, a musical instrument.

"The fourth was espoused to a high lord *Takefusa*. She was a very sympathetic lady, and was very accomplished in playing on the *koto*.

"The fifth became the wife of Konoe-Moto-Mitsu-Ko. Her beautiful complexion was compared to a crystal covered by a thin veil. Her father gave her the name of ' *Soto-rihime* ' (the Princess of Transparency). She was a celebrated poetess.

"The sixth was married to Lord *Nobutaka*. Her glossy hair and rosy cheeks were more beautiful than the jewels she wore, and brighter than the light of the moon, and her presence spread lustre all around. She was famous for her painting and poetry and also excelled in the art of making poetry in company; was clever at making ornamental cards, and had a tender and generous heart. She was devoted to Buddhism and entered the temple to serve Buddha, making offerings, burning incense and reading prayers all day long.

"The seventh daughter had no particular accomplishments, but she was a paragon of beauty.

"The eighth was married to the Lord *Arifusa*. She painted well, tied ornamental cords cleverly, and her handwriting was very skillful. She was a good composer of poetry as well as prose, though these latter accomplishments were rarely possessed by women. She painted illustrations of a hundred poems on the sliding paper doors. She also did the writing of the poems herself to the great admiration of the Emperor for her rare talent."

It seems to us that in this record these ladies were too much praised, but by this we can see what accomplishments were learned by ladies in ancient times.

During the thirteenth century *Sohekimon-in*, *Kunaikio*, *Ukiodaiu*, etc., were Court ladies noted for painting.

" *Niwa-no-Oshie* " (mentioned in the preface and also in the "Women in Literature") was compiled in the last part of the thirteenth century by *Abutsuni*, and was dedicated to her daughter to assist her in her education. In it the authoress says: " Although painting may not be an indispensable accomplishment, still, it is well you should learn it to be able to paint beautiful portraits, or to illustrate narratives and other things in your leisure hours."

Such was the general impression in regard to women studying painting. After the time of the *Ashikaga* government, the Imperial power was very much decreased, and the consequence was that but little was heard of accomplished women in the Court.

The Shogun *Ashikaga*, however, gave great encouragement to the fine arts, and this was the time when a great many famous artists appeared; and among them were some women who gained the highest name in this art.

*Chiyo-jo*, the daughter of *Tosa Mitsunobu*, an artist of great celebrity, became the wife of *Motonobu*, who was the ancestor of the Kano family of artists, and she gained great fame as an artist.

When the *Tokugawa* family came into power, literature, which had fallen into a low state, greatly improved, and literary women and female artists again made their appearance.

*Yukinobu*, a lady relative of the famous *Tannyu*, was a most talented artist.

Painting is in a flourishing condition at the present day. It is taught in the primary as well as in the higher schools for girls; there are also many lady students who go to private studios to study with famous artists.

A fine arts society called "*Nippon Bijutsu-kio-kwai*," was recently organized. The members consist of noted artists. The object of this organization is to encourage the fine arts. Public exhibitions are also given of members' paintings at stated times. A chosen committee criticise their work, and medals, certificates or prizes are awarded to the most skillful artists.

They sometimes borrow from different persons the choicest paintings of ancient as well as present times, and arrange loan exhibitions so the students may benefit by them. These exhibitions have been honored by frequent visits from Their Imperial Majesties, the Emperor and the Empress. When they recognize a work of true merit they often become its purchaser, and the painting is sent to the palace.

Above all other favors conferred by Their Imperial Majesties upon the artists, the most gracious one is to ask one or more of them to use his or her brush while in the Imperial presence. A few years ago at one of Her Imperial Majesty's visits at the exhibition, the following ladies painted before Her Majesty the Empress:

| | |
|---|---|
| Koai Takemura, | Kakei Atomi, |
| Shohin Noguchi, | Hokoku Takabayashi, |
| Giokushi Atomi, | Seisui Okuzawa, |
| Seikoku Sakuma, | Masu Tanaka. |

Her Majesty, our beloved Empress, is most clever and intelligent, well learned in literature and poetry. Moreover she takes great interest in painting. She is known to take her brush in hand and to paint beautifully. She gives great encouragement by her visits to the exhibitions, and also does much for the improvement of the art, and there is every prospect of painting being largely developed during the present reign of Their Imperial Majesties.

### APPLICATION OF THE ART OF PAINTING.

The art of painting is applied to a variety of uses, viz., porcelain, lacquer, gold lacquer work, inlaid work, sculpture, designs for weaving, dyeing, embroidery, raised silk work and other ornamentations of various kinds.

As weaving, embroidery, raised silk work, etc., are mostly done by women, they learn painting to prepare themselves for these occupations.

For particulars in regard to the work or industries of women, the reader is referred to the chapters upon "Women's Industries."

# CHAPTER VIII.

## PRESENT OR MEIJI PERIOD, CHARITIES AND EDUCATION.

The older women were what they were in consequence of "The Three Obediences," the rule of Confucius referred to at some length in the introductory chapter. All the laws and customs that had anything to do with the relation of women to men, and to other women, were based upon this rule. No wonder, therefore, if it was considered the height of womanly virtue to be absolutely obedient.

The activity of women was limited to the domestic circle. They were of no importance outside of their families. They had nothing to say or to do with the public lives of their husbands. It was derogatory to their character to mingle in any public affairs, be it ever so little.

But this state of indifference outside of the domestic circle is now gone, let us hope never to return. The tide of Western civilization has reached our shores. Philosophical educators have declared the advisability of raising the social status of our women. To this idea a few of the more brave and enlightened have responded by calling upon their sisters to extend their interests beyond the home circle and make themselves recognized as real members of society and not merely of families.

The result is there are already not a few women who are earning independent livelihoods, not because they are pressed by poverty, but simply to practically prove how well their sex can do in professional life. What is of still more consequence, if not of more benefit to society at large, there has come out from her secluded home many a woman who is now taking an important part in educational and philanthropic affairs.

## Women in Public Affairs in the Meiji Period.

The tendency of women towards an enlargement of their sphere of action briefly alluded to above, has given rise to a number of educational and charitable institutions under their management. Some of the more important are the *Fujin-Kyoiku Kwai* (Women's Educational Society), the *Fujin Jizen Kwai* (Women's Charity Bazaar Association), the *Tokyo Jikei Byoin* (Tokyo Charity Hospital) and the *Tokyo Ikuji-in* (Tokyo Orphanage).

In all these Her Imperial Majesty, our wise and most gracious Empress, takes the lead. There has not been a notable stand taken by women that has been for the public benefit but that the Empress in the kindness of her heart has not either directly or indirectly given it her patronage.

When the Kagoshima war broke out in 1877, she sent an immense quantity of lint pledgets of her own preparation for the use of the wounded soldiers. She every year practices silk culture in her palace in order to share in the labors of her poor people. Whenever the charity bazaar is held, she visits it and makes large purchases. The cause of education is not less dear to her heart, and she often visits the schools for girls, the Peeresses School, the Girls' Normal School, the Girls' High School, and even others of less note, not to merely present herself before them, but to make a close examination which might only be expected of a school inspector. She also visits the Tokyo Charity Hospital, and speaks a kind word to the patients and presents them with gifts. Such an illustrious example can but be followed by the ladies of the upper classes, and does much to enlarge the sphere of the usefulness and activity of women. The establishment of various educational and benevolent institutions, and the publishing of various magazines by women, have done not a little towards determining the direction in which the women of the Meiji period are taking rapid steps in progress.

Shall women interest themselves in political affairs? This is a question yet unanswered in every quarter of the globe. As for Japan, her customs and her circumstances direct us to answer it in the negative. Household cares and such public affairs as appertain to the minor charities and female education, are well suited to the feminine nature, while unbecoming to the stronger sex. It is therefore our opinion, and that of most of our sisters, that public affairs, except those mentioned above, should not be engaged in by women, especially in all affairs pertaining to politics.

We do not hesitate to own that our women are not yet far advanced in public usefulness, but it is not a little consolatory to say that they have lately been placed in the right path of progress through the sterling efforts of some noble and learned women under the great leadership of Her Imperial Majesty, the Empress.

### CHARITIES.

In woman's sphere of public activity, charities and the correction of such social evils as the law or religion has little or no control over seem the most womanly. Japan is to be much congratulated that her women have come to a knowledge of this duty and are taking steps to make themselves instrumental in doing good to their country. They have established in various parts of the Empire health and temperance societies, associations for the improvement of social manners and customs, and also for the abolition of licensed prostitution. They have also done much to purify the stage and street manners by inducing scholars and composers to make good plays and songs. They have not yet reaped much benefit from the various associations, but have very bright prospects before them.

The public charity in which Japanese women have thus far shown the greatest interest is the relief of the indigent. Hospitals for needy patients have been established and asylums for orphans and other poor children, all of which have gained the warmest sympathy of the public. It is reasonably expected that similar institutions will be established in many of the provincial towns at no distant future.

We have now many benevolent institutions founded and managed by ladies' associations and individual women. A few of them will be enumerated.

### I. THE TOKYO CHARITY HOSPITAL.

The Tokyo Charity Hospital was established in 1887. It was and is under the direction of Her Majesty, the Empress and a ladies' association called the "Tokyo Charity Hospital Association." It is managed directly by a staff of functionaries, consisting of a president, ten directresses, fourteen consulting doctors, a chief doctor, an assistant chief doctor, and a number of ordinary doctors and secretaries and clerks. The directresses, who are all ladies of high rank, are selected from among the supporters of the institution by the Empress herself, and the other principal functionaries are nominated by the association under the direction of Her Majesty, the Empress. The present chief doctor, his assistant chief doctors and consulting doctors, are all celebrities of the profession.

The hospital was first started by a number of ladies who formed themselves into an association called "The Benevolent Society" (Jizen Kwai), from whom the management of the hospital was soon severed, and it was then placed under the patronage of Her Majesty, the Empress.

Soon after its opening the institution, too true to its nature, becoming cramped for means to carry on its work, obtained relief and encouragement from Their Imperial Majesties, the Emperor and the Empress and the Empress Dowager.

The former gave a magnificent donation of 20,000 yen, and the others an annuity of 600 yen. Following these illustrious examples, the members of the association did all in their power only too gladly. They held a grand council and resolved to call for public aid to increase the permanent fund of the hospital, also to invite each member to contribute from one to five yen per month towards ordinary expenses, and to hold a charity bazaar each October, one-half of the profits secured on the occasion to be devoted to augment the said fund, and the other half to be given to other charitable institutions.

The fund of the hospital is now estimated at 17,000 yen. This is kept as a reserved fund. The monthly expenditures which vary from six to seven hundred yen, are defrayed by contributions from the members of the association.

More than a thousand years ago the Empress Komyo founded a similar hospital on a much smaller scale.

This society was founded upon Buddhist doctrines of benevolence in 1779 by a number of devout women, represented by such persons as the Princess Mori, Marchioness Tokugawa, Viscountesses Forio and Miura, Baroness Kagitori and several other ladies of no less celebrity. The Fukuden (happy field) Society is still a well-known Buddhist association established for charitable purposes. The special object of the society is the support and management of its orphanage at No. 103 Azabu, Kogai-cho, Tokyo. In 1891 the ladies of this society did much for the relief of distressed children whose parents had been killed in the great Gifu-Aichi earthquake.

The children in the orphanage are all taught in the elements of a common school education, and when they reach 12 years of age are taught some kind of useful industry. At 15 years they are put in some suitable position to become nurses, midwives, weavers, etc.

### III.   CHRISTIAN BENEVOLENT SOCIETIES.

There are quite a number of Christian women's societies, as scarcely a church in the whole country, but has some kind of benevolent society attached to it. Perhaps the best organized and regulated among them is the Fujin Kyofu Kwai, established in 1886 by Mrs. Kaji-ko Yajima, of the Sakurai girls' school, and over thirty other ladies. The origin of this society was the visit of Mrs. Mary C. Leavitt of the Women's Temperance Society of America, to this country. She came here in June, 1882, and gave many lectures, both in Yokohama and Tokyo, upon the subject of temperance. Mrs. Yajima listened to the American lady and was greatly moved. She then directed all her energies, in conjunction with thirty-eight other ladies, towards establishing a sister association to the American society, whose messenger had so strongly influenced her. Mrs. Yajima's exertions were at last crowned with success, the formal opening of the society taking place on the 6th December, 1888. Its members are over five hundred at the present writing. Its aims are:

First.   To improve public morality.

Second. To correct or eradicate all sorts of social evils, especially drinking and smoking.

Third. To relieve the distressed.

Fourth. To change manners and customs for the better.

Fifth. To improve sanitary conditions.

Sixth. To put moral education on a better basis.

Seventh. To increase the real happiness of human life.

Each member of the society is pledged to live a pure life herself, and to direct her energies towards the attainment of one or more of the above mentioned objects. The annual income, consisting of fees and donations from the members, amounts to about four hundred yen. The charitable works hitherto accomplished by the society are many, of which the following are the best known:

First. When large portions of Wakayama, Okayama and Fukuoka prefectures suffered from inundations in 1889, the society sent a large quantity of old clothing and a sum of 250 yen to such of the sufferers as needed help. It is to be observed that a portion of the amount was raised by means of a concert.

Second. At the time of the great earthquake of 1891, a number of nurses were sent to the shaken districts with instructions to give their services to the injured for six weeks. They also opened their purses and wardrobes to relieve the distressed.

### EDUCATION OF WOMEN.
#### 1868-70.

As early as the first year of the restoration, the government saw objections in restricting the education of women to such branches of learning as were only needed in the management of domestic affairs, and in the new educational code which was soon promulgated included an educational system for girls, and sent some promising ones abroad to be educated and thus secure some able leaders in the new school system when they returned. The people also of our land fully acknowledged the importance of a more expanded and enlightened education for girls than that formerly in vogue. The result of all this thought and preparation has been quite satisfactory, when we make due allowance for the shortness of time the new system has been in working order.

The number of female teachers now employed in educational institutions is about five thousand, and the girls attending school number nearly a million. The graduates of the various schools from 1881–1889, inclusive, are estimated at 354,392. This number is by no means large compared with our population of over forty million, but when we consider that all these girls have been educated to appear on the social stage, each in her appropriate character, we may rest assured that they will be of great benefit to the future of Japan.

Of late the study of medicine and nursing has become quite a popular profession for women and there are already a number of lady doctors and nurses who are possessed of scientific knowledge. Until a few years ago nearly all the higher schools for girls were public institutions, but more recently there has sprung up many private ones, proving that education for women is making rapid progress.

Kindergarten schools are on the increase in all parts of the empire.

### I. THE PEERESSES SCHOOL.

This school for the daughters of noblemen was formerly a department of the Gakushiu-in, now a school for the sons of peers. In September, 1885, it was disconnected from the boys' institution and on the fifth of the following October the work of instruction was commenced in its new buildings. On the thirteenth of November next, Her Imperial Majesty, the Empress, visited and formally opened it, making a long speech in regard to its usefulness and the importance of education in general.

This school was established in accordance with the wishes of H. I. M. the Empress, and is under the control of the Imperial Household Department. Its object is to educate the daughters of the nobility, physically, intellectually and morally so they may be well fitted to their high stations in life. It admits any daughter belonging to a noble family above 6 and under 18 years of age. It has four different courses of study:

First. A common school course of six years.

Second. A middle school course of six years.

Third. A post-graduate course, in which classic Japanese, one or more modern languages, drawing and music are made the objects of special study.

Fourth. A special course in which such students as have outgrown the other courses are instructed in a few essential subjects.

The number of teachers and assistants, including the president, is forty-seven, and that of the students 362.

## II. THE HIGHER NORMAL SCHOOL FOR GIRLS.

This institution was first founded in July, 1874, under the name of the Tokyo Female Normal School (*Tokyo Joshi Shihan Gakko*) and was given its present name in March, 1890.

In April, 1876, a preparatory department was attached to it, as so few girls were found having enough learning to enter upon the regular normal course. In June of the same year a kindergarten was started in this school, and two years later a common school department was added to give the students in the normal course practical training in the work of teaching. A department was also added to train students as teachers in kindergartens throughout the Empire. This department was abolished in 1880, and the study of kindergarten training was added to the curriculum of the normal students. At the same time classic Japanese, etiquette and domestic industries enlarged the same curriculum. In July, 1882, the preparatory department was abolished and a higher girls' school department was added. In August, 1885, the several departments were amalgamated under the name of Tokyo Normal School (*Tokyo Shihan Gakko*). In March, 1890, it was again made independent under the present name, "*Joshi Koto Shihan Gakko*."

The present purpose of the institution is to give good teachers to normal and higher schools for girls, and also to kindergartens. The students are selected from among those girls who have finished a two years' course in ordinary normal schools, and those who have passed an equivalent examination. A number of such girls are nominated by the governor of each prefecture, and from among them the directors of the normal school select a certain number. The regular course runs four years. The number of hours devoted to instruction is thirty-one per week. The teachers number forty-eight, and the students ninety-seven.

The expenses of the students are defrayed by the government. The graduates are each bound to perform school work for five full years from the day of the reception of the diploma, and that teaching must be done at a certain school indicated by the Department of Education for the first three years.

Up to March, 1892, the number of graduates have been 266 in the lower department, and forty-five in the higher department. Most of them are already engaged in educational work.

### III.   THE CORPORATE INDUSTRIAL SCHOOL FOR GIRLS.

This is a private enterprise for teaching girls in such industrial arts as are suitable for them, together with the essential elements of learning.

The industries taught are sewing, knitting, embroidery, flower making and painting. Lessons are also given in practical ethics, reading, writing, arithmetic, domestic industries and the elements of science. English is also taught to such girls as may desire to learn it. There are two courses of study, respectively called the "A" and the "B" course, the former of which runs four years and the latter three years. The hours of instruction are seven per day. The authorities, including the director, number thirty-two, and the number of pupils 344. The present director is Mr. Tegima Sei-ichi, who is now in Chicago on official duty at the World's Columbian Exposition. This school was established in September, 1886, and has since sent forth 372 graduates. A few noteworthy facts connected with the institution may be mentioned:

First. Its authorities and students contributed both money and labor when the great Gifu-Aichi earthquake occurred, and sent 321 cotton flannel shirts to the poor sufferers.

Second. Once every year many ladies and gentlemen are invited to inspect the methods of instruction and the students' manual productions which are then sold at reasonable rates. Last year when the third of such occasions was celebrated the visitors numbered 10,000 and the proceeds of the sales amounted to 384 *yen*. ·

Third.   The institution has a money-saving system which is to deposit one-half of the profits secured by the sale of manufactured articles at the savings office of the Teishinsho (Department of Communications).   Such savings have now grown to the respectable sum of 244 *yen*.

Fourth.   On the 12th of April, 1889, Her Imperial Majesty, the Empress, visited the school, made a minute in. spection of the various articles made by the students and had sent to her palace such as pleased her.   The school also received a gift of 200 yen from the Imperial hand.

Fifth.   On the 29th of October, 1891, and the 14th of January 1892, His Majesty, the Emperor, sent a chamberlain to the school to inquire after its condition and to instruct the authorities to send some of the articles manufactured by the students to the Imperial palace to be honored by his inspection.   To the credit and pleasure of the girls, many of the articles sent to the palace were never returned to their hands.

There are other public and private schools of much importance.   Of these the most famous is the Atomi school for young ladies, established in 1875 by Miss Atomi Kwakei, which has already graduated 3,000 girls.   Among others of note are some founded by Christians of the various denominations.

As may be seen by glancing over these pages, education for the women of this country is now in a fair way of progress. We do not entertain a shadow of doubt as to its producing beneficial results.

The educational philosophers of Japan are now studying how to unite the intellectual methods of Western systems with the teachings of Oriental morality, which has hitherto preserved the feminine virtues, from the days of old down to the present time.   Whether they will succeed in basing them on the history and peculiarities of Japanese custom, has much to do with the future of the Empire.

We here append a table of the present educational institutions for female students, according to the latest reports (1890–92), published by the Monbusho, or the Educational Department of the Imperial Government.

| INSTITUTIONS. | NUMBERS OF SCHOOLS. | | | | | | FEMALE STUDENTS. | | FEMALE TEACHERS. | |
|---|---|---|---|---|---|---|---|---|---|---|
| | Gov't. | | Public. | | Private. | | | | | |
| | 1890 | 1891 | 1890 | 1891 | 1890 | 1891 | 1890 | 1891 | 1890 | 1891 |
| Higher Female Schools........ | 1 | 1 | 7 | 7 | 23 | 21 | 3,115 | 2,768 | 153 | 166 |
| Female Dep'ts of Ordinary Normal Schools.......... | .... | .... | 28 | 27 | .... | .... | 885 | 838 | 45 | 47 |
| Chinese and Japanese Schools (*Public*) ...... | .... | .... | .... | .... | .... | .... | 412 | 615 | 31 | 36 |
| Chinese and Japanese Schools (*Private*).... | .... | .... | .... | .... | .... | .... | 5,677 | 5,492 | 127 | 159 |
| English Schools (*Private*).... | .... | .... | .... | .... | .... | .... | 2,495 | 1,248 | 121 | 110 |
| French Schools (*Private*).... | .... | .... | .... | .... | .... | .... | 36 | ...... | 4 | ...... |
| German Schools (*Private*).... | .... | .... | .... | .... | .... | .... | 3 | 17 | ...... | 2 |
| Russian Schools (*Private*).... | .... | .... | .... | .... | .... | .... | .... | 2 | ...... | ...... |
| Medical Schools (*Private*).... | .... | .... | .... | .... | .... | .... | 10 | ...... | ...... | ...... |
| Pharmaceutical Schools (*Private*).......... | .... | .... | .... | .... | .... | .... | 3 | 6 | ...... | ...... |
| Commercial Schools (*Private*). | .... | .... | .... | .... | .... | .... | 23 | 12 | ...... | ...... |
| Mathematical Schools (*Private*) | .... | .... | .... | .... | .... | .... | 276 | 325 | 3 | 2 |
| Bookkeepers' Schools (*Private*) | .... | .... | .... | .... | .... | .... | 40 | 50 | 2 | 1 |
| Writing Schools (*Private*)..... | .... | .... | .... | .... | .... | .... | 1,285 | 1,381 | 17 | 14 |
| Painters' Schools (*Private*).... | .... | .... | .... | .... | .... | .... | 24 | 13 | ...... | ...... |
| Industrial Schools (*Private*)... | .... | .... | .... | .... | .... | .... | 4,407 | 5,504 | 173 | 218 |
| Midwifery Schools (*Private*).. | .... | .... | .... | .... | .... | 38 | 308 | 364 | 22 | 28 |
| Chinese, English and Mathematical Schools (*Private*).. | .... | .... | .... | .... | .... | .... | 344 | 909 | 35 | 52 |
| Music Schools (*Private*)....... | .... | .... | .... | .... | .... | .... | 97 | 99 | 4 | 2 |
| Sick Nurses' Schools (*Private*) | .... | .... | .... | .... | .... | .... | 28 | 21 | 2 | 4 |
| Science Schools (*Private*)..... | .... | .... | .... | .... | 1 | 1 | 29 | 15 | ... | ... |
| Kindergarten System Schools (*Private*).......... | .... | .... | .... | .... | 2 | 2 | 20 | 33 | 3 | 5 |
| Technological Schools(*Private*) | .... | .... | .... | .... | .... | .... | ...... | 13 | ...... | 2 |
| Literature Schools (*Private*).. | .... | .... | .... | .... | .... | .... | ...... | 36 | ...... | .. |
| Shampooers' Schools (*Private*). | .... | .... | .... | .... | .... | .... | ...... | 3 | ...... | ...... |
| Common Schools............. | .... | .... | .... | .... | .... | .... | 915,238 | 917,270 | 3,738 | 4,149 |

| | Public and Private. | | Infants. | | Instructresses. | |
|---|---|---|---|---|---|---|
| | 1890 | 1891 | 1890 | 1891 | 1890 | 1891 |
| Kindergartens............... | 138 | 147 | 7,486 | 8,662 | 271 | 317 |